The Runaway

A memoir of a life on the run

By, Joy Sidebottom

While every precaution has been taken in the preparation of this book, the publisher assumes no responsibility for errors or omissions, or for damages resulting from the use of the information contained herein.

THE RUNAWAY

First edition. September 27, 2023.

Copyright © 2023 Joy Sidebottom.

ISBN: 979-8223348566

Written by Joy Sidebottom.

Table of Contents

A special thank you to my family and friends who helped read the manuscript and gave such good feedback. (Chris, Hilton, Neta, my mom, Barbara, David, Leanne, Duane, Aaron, and Avery) I especially want to thank Chris Enss for helping me believe this was even possible, to begin with! A very special thank you to my wonderful husband for supporting me, my Pastor for his editing and insight, all my Juvenile Hall kids who told me to write this, my daughter Grace for her artistic input on the cover design, and my daughter Avery for being the final set of eyes and my creative writing expert. This was a long time coming and I couldn't have done it without all of the support and encouragement. Thank you all from the bottom of my heart!

This book is dedicated to the memory of Matthew Stephen Richards and to any who may have lost their way. May it give you hope that God has the power to change any life; may it bring light to your dark situation; and may you see that His grace has been pursuing you all along, directing you to the road that would eventually lead you to Him.

Introduction

This is a true story. It is not a pretty one. It is not a fairy tale...but a nightmare that was my reality for too many years. In my story, things don't work out perfectly (or at least what I perceive as perfect)...they're not supposed to.

This is Joy Sidebottom's story. This is my story...

...of being a girl born in a broken home.

...of succumbing to the lure of the drug world.

...of surviving mental, physical and drug abuse.

...of running away from home, the police, and an abuser.

...of surviving kidnapping and the influences of darkness

...of rising from addiction and defeat.

...of claiming the gift of freedom and physical healing.

...of finding, then pursuing grace.

...of telling God's story of mercy, grace and goodness

...from a broken, wounded, and drug-addicted runaway

to a woman of purpose and value.

My story is intended to bear witness of the power of God's ability to change any life no matter how broken. My story doesn't end there because my story, like yours, is still being written. Mine also bears witness of the power of God's grace to change a person and the power of His grace to strengthen a person, to test her, to sustain her in the face of life's greatest tragedies, to bless her beyond measure, and to gently lead her on through the journey of life.

I pray that as you read my story you will be able to see your own story much clearer.

All my thoughts are in italics and Bible verses from the New King James Version (NKJV) or the English Standard Version (ESV).

Chapter 1
Evil's Pursuit

"The wicked flee when no one pursues,
but the righteous are bold as a lion." Proverbs 28:1 (NKJV)

November 1993, Grass Valley, California

HOW DID I GET HERE? I am alone in the dark, lying in the mud, gasping for each breath, terrified that at any moment they will find me. Afraid and unable to move, my mind raced through the events of the night.

It wasn't supposed to happen like this; it was supposed to be a simple drug run. Why did I go with him? I don't even know this guy! I must be crazy. Out of all the tweakers in the house, for some reason I volunteered to go—not just because it sounded exciting, but I had never been on a motorcycle before. I had not done many things before; I was only fourteen!

However, when your life consists of chasing one high to the next, you're willing to do what it takes to keep the supply of drugs flowing. In a house full of like minded people, someone has to be the one to go into the real world, find a dealer, buy the goods and make it back safely to the nest full of hungry addicts waiting to consume the score. When "Red" (the guy with the motorcycle and nicknamed by his hair color) found a dealer with the goods we were looking for, he then asked if someone could go with him. Eager and excited to get more drugs while also getting to go on an adventure, I volunteered. Of course I had to lie about riding on a motorcycle before and just acted like I had the experience needed to go on our mission. Yet nothing could have prepared me for that ride.

It was an extremely cold night. I don't even know what time it was. High on methamphetamine, I had lost all sense of time in that drug house. Red probably knew that I had never really been on a motorcycle, so he gave me some pointers on how to lean with the bike when we went around turns; then he handed me a helmet, and we were off. It was not a long drive to where we were going. We got to the place, bought the drugs, and then left—very simple, all according to plan. We drove off the road somewhere into the woods so we could test out the stuff before going back to the drug house. (one of the perks of going on the mission) We each snorted a long line of the meth. It seemed like good dope; then we took off. Everyone was eagerly waiting for us to return with the drugs so we didn't dare waste any time.

The silence of the night was disturbed all around us as we drove through sleeping neighborhoods. There was no turning down the volume on a motorcycle, no sneaking by so we hurried through town. All the houses were dark except for the yellow glow illuminating from the street lights. I was lost in the excitement of the moment and the feeling of having accomplished our dangerous mission when I saw a car up ahead. My eyes wouldn't focus on the shape of the car; they kept blurring until it was closer. The outline became clear; it was a cop! He was driving very slowly in the lane opposite of us, too slowly. Instantly, fear and panic gripped my heart. The driver of the motorcycle said to me, "If that cop turns around and stops us, do you want me to risk my ass and let you off or keep going?"

Without hesitation I said, "Keep going." I had arrest warrants for running away from home and violating my probation, so I was not interested in going to juvenile hall that night. "Keep going" were two very simple words spoken in haste that almost cost me my life. We did not make it too much farther down the road when, sure enough, that cop turned around and started to follow us. The pounding of my heart reached my throat, and I was tingling all over from the adrenaline surging throughout my body as I anticipated what was about to happen. Expecting my driver to take off at any moment, I held on tightly.

The lights started flashing, but we didn't stop. The chase was on! I had no idea how we would outrun the cops but I hoped somehow we could. We were driving down a straight stretch of highway 20, so it was a perfect place to take off. Before I knew what was happening, Red pulled the motorcycle over! *What happened to keep going?*

"What are you doing?" I asked him.

Just then, the officer spoke over his loudspeaker, "Turn off the bike!"

He just sat there, not moving.

Again the cop said, "Turn off the bike! This is Officer Jones of the Grass Valley police department, and I order you to turn off your bike!"

Accelerating and turning the bike around all at once, the driver went back in the direction we had just come, passing the police officer on the side of the road. He gunned it so hard that I was nearly knocked off and was going so fast that the air caught my helmet and started pulling me back. My heart was racing as I tried to lean into him, but the wind kept pulling me. The force of the wind in the helmet and the acceleration of the bike was so strong I thought I would fly off the bike at any moment. It would mean a certain and painful death for me, so I continued to hold on with all my strength. As the pursuit continued, he got off the freeway and started weaving the bike through the downtown streets. Thankfully, there were not very many cars out since it was the middle of the night, so we were able to drive through the streets at high speeds. As the passenger, I could only hold on tightly; I had no control and did not even know when he would speed up or slow down. My hands turned numb, and I began to wonder how long I could even hang on. Then all of a sudden, they were on us! First two, then three cop cars! They had caught up so quickly!

At one point, I looked down and saw the bumper of a cop car within a foot of me! *They're going to kill us!* I thought to myself. In that moment, it was no longer an adventure but a danger so real that I may not survive it. I readjusted my hands to hold on tighter, then shut my eyes. With every turn, I leaned with the bike. There was no escaping this nightmare. Even with my eyes shut, all I could see were red flashing lights. I looked up—a roadblock! Parked sideways, two sheriff's cars blocked the road. *Now the Sheriff's department had joined the pursuit! No way we are making it out of this alive!* We slowed down, then weaved between them, and took off at such force that I almost flew off again! He drove through street after street until finally he couldn't see them behind us. He parked the bike in a small neighborhood then yelled, "RUN!" I never expected him to park and run! I was stunned, almost paralyzed with fear. Finally, my feet started to move...but my helmet! I couldn't get my helmet off! I could hardly see! I yelled for him to help me, but he was gone. I ran across someone's front yard, jumped a fence, then finally got my helmet off! It was so dark; my heart was racing, and I was so afraid.

You have to run, Joy! You have to run! I kept telling myself. I ran through another yard, jumped another fence, then another and another! I just kept going. Suddenly after jumping a wooden fence, I was next to a house; there were bushes, and it was dark. Exhausted, I couldn't keep running, so I crawled onto the wet, cold ground under the bushes. Groping with my hands along the ground in the dark, I felt a pile of hoses coiled up. Curling up in the coiled hoses, I held my knees to my chest and tried to hold still. I was panting so heavily the cold air was stinging my lungs with every breath. *They will hear me!* My heart pounded so hard I thought it would explode! Terrified, I shut my eyes tight for a moment, as though somehow I could disappear and escape the situation.

Opening my eyes, a flash of light caught my attention. *Is that a spotlight? A helicopter! They are going to find me!* The red and blue lights danced in the shadows all around me. *Calm down, Joy! You have to calm down!* Thinking about the situation, I was reminded of one of my favorite movies, *The Fugitive.* I thought about the main character, played by Harrison Ford, running from the cops and hiding in a pile of leaves on the riverbank. Suddenly my nerves began to calm and my breathing was slowing down. It was helping! So, I kept thinking about the movie to distract myself until I heard footsteps, leaves crunching. *They're getting closer.* I could hear an officer's radio clicking on and off. Footsteps, leaves crunching, closer and closer. *Don't move Joy! He will see me...this is it! I will serve more time for running than I would have for my warrants! What have I done? Why did I say "Keep going"?* Footsteps, leaves, radio clicks. *He is now on the other side of the fence I am hiding behind! At any moment he will open the gate and it will be all over.* Footsteps, leaves crunching, radio clicking. *Wait! It's getting farther away! The footsteps are going the other way!*

A sense of relief washed over me, but I continued to hold still. Lying there curled up in a ball, I watched the lights dance in the trees; the spotlight would shine, then be gone. The dark shadows surrounded me in the mud, but the trees seemed alive as they bounced with flashes of light. I don't know how long I lay there watching the lights. My eyelids got so heavy. I had never been so tired. After the adrenaline wore off, my body relaxed, and I passed out.

I thought only a few minutes had passed when I woke up. I could still see the lights flashing through the trees as they had before. Now I was shaking; my clothes were soaked. I was so cold. *Wait, Joy; they are still there.* I told myself. *But I am so cold.* I argued. It felt like knives were cutting into my flesh, and my teeth were chattering uncontrollably. *If I stay here, I will die! I would rather go to jail than freeze to death!* I willed myself to move; my body felt so stiff. Every joint ached and trembled as I made my way from the security of my dark, hiding place and moved toward the lights. The reality of what I was doing sunk in, and I imagined getting shot before being able to raise my hands in surrender.

I put my hands up before even making it out of the bushes. Not sure what would happen next, I stepped from the cover of brush and waited for the police to rush in and throw me to the ground. When I looked up, there was nothing—no flashing lights, no cop cars, nothing but an empty street in a quiet neighborhood. *Were the cops really gone? Were they ever really there? Did I imagine this? Perhaps a hallucination from the drugs I had taken?* Everything was a blur; I had no way of knowing what was real and what was not, but the freezing, wet, cold was very real; it was all I could feel. *I can't stop shaking. I am so cold! Where am I? I don't recognize the street, the houses; I am lost.*

Willing my feet to move, I started walking. The cold, night air pierced my lungs, and I was still shaking uncontrollably. *I have to get warm!* There was a house up ahead that had its lights on. I could see a woman inside, so I knocked on the door.

"Who is it?" she said through the door.

"Please help me; I am so cold," came my trembling reply.

"I am scared to open the door," she said cautiously. "Were you on a motorcycle?" she questioned.

Stunned that she knew about it, I quickly answered, "What motorcycle? Please help me. I ran away from my boyfriend. He was hurting me, and now I am lost." I had been running all right, and I was lost. She slowly opened the door and looked at me. I did look beaten up, so she reluctantly let me in. I warmed myself by the heater while she got ready for work. I used the restroom and drank a cup of coffee. She offered to give me a ride home. *Home? A strange and foreign word. I had no home.* I just wanted to get back to the drug house, but I didn't even know the name of the street that it was on. I didn't even know whose house it actually was. *If she took me to town I could find my way from there.*

Once she finished getting ready for work, we got into her car to leave. As she drove out of her neighborhood, I recognized some of the streets from the previous night. She told me about a high speed chase the cops had with a motorcycle the night before. I made up more details to my made-up story of running from a boyfriend. Then I saw it—the house! We drove right past it! I was only a few blocks away from it all along! I could have walked back if I had known where I was! I didn't want her to know where I was going just in case she didn't believe my story, so I had her drive me a few blocks away and drop me off. Then I walked back.

When I knocked on the door of the house, there was a long pause before it opened. No one could believe that I had made it back! They seemed amazed to see me at first. Then the shock wore off quickly and turned into a deep paranoia as they bombarded me with questions: "How did you get away?" "Did you get away?" "Were you arrested, then snitched and are now bringing the cops here?"

I told my story though their suspicions were not satisfied. I was surrounded by tweakers who did not believe my crazy but true story. Then Red the driver of the motorcycle walked into the room! "You got away?" he exclaimed. "I thought they caught you for sure!" I had thought the same thing about him. We shared our stories of escape. The tension and paranoia was thick and heavy in the room as the stories were too unbelievable.

By the whispers and bugged out eyes looking at me, I knew I was not welcomed there anymore. I felt betrayed. I thought of my time and contributions there at the house. I had cleaned the disgusting kitchen just so I could cook a meal for everyone. I had no money, so I had gone to the food bank and gotten food just so I could feed these people who looked like they hadn't eaten in a week! I hadn't even known them and had tried to help them, had tried to bring them a little happiness, had tried to be accepted. Now, was there no loyalty? No, there is no loyalty among tweakers. Every addict is out for himself. I should know; I was one. To whom but myself was I loyal? That is an ugly part of being an addict. You can only truly care about yourself—self-indulgence, self-preservation above all.

I took a shower, changed my clothes, and left the house. I didn't even know whose house it was. I just knew I would not be going back.

Chapter 2
Self-Made Prison

"There is a way that seems right to a man,
but its end is the way of death."
Proverbs 14:12 (NKJV)

September 1994, Grass Valley, California

HOW DID I GET HERE? I am standing in front of a corpse. This person looks dead. Her eyes are deeply sunk into their sockets. She is so pale, so thin; I can see her ribs. She is covered in sores; she looks like she is on the brink of death. She is moving, but there is no life in her—like the walking dead. I don't even recognize this person. How can this be me? I am supposed to be young and pretty. The person I see in the mirror has no beauty, no youth, no life in her. She looks old and dead. What have I done? How has this become me?

This drug is killing me—slowly killing me. I hate it; yet, I love it. I desperately want it; yet, I hate what it is doing to me, but I need it. I can't function right without it. I long for it. It keeps me numb. It keeps me from feeling all the pain, the overwhelming pain—until it wears off. I just can't let it wear off, but look at me now. I am alive, but I am dead. I feel free when I am high, but really I have no freedom. I am in prison...meth is my slave master. I do its bidding. I serve it with all I am. It is a cruel master. It has taken everything from me! I have nothing left: no family, no joy, no friends, no possessions. It possesses me! I wasn't always like this. How did I get here? How did I become like this?

When I was a little girl of six years old in California I had many hopes and dreams for the future. My imagination ran wild! I also loved fairy tales and dreamed I was in one every chance I got. Pretending to be Cinderella was a favorite whenever I had to do my chores! I loved to pretend, to act out the movies and books I had read, to dress up and dream, and to pretend I was in another life and not in my own—that I was another person and not me. My dreams included becoming an actress, an author, and an archaeologist...nothing to do with each other except the letters they start with, but, nevertheless, all things I wanted to do in my future. I wanted a good future. My dreams also included the day that my daddy would come and rescue me. He was my long awaited prince who would save me from the villains and take me to a land far, far away where all my dreams would come true. Only, life is nothing like a fairy tale. Is it?

One night in 1989 when I was ten years old, I was home alone with my older brother Matt when the phone rang. Immediately, I ran up the stairs to my room so I could secretly listen in on the conversation. My mom had recently put a telephone in my room, and I was so excited to get to use it, so excited to have a real telephone in my own room. It even had a mute button, so it was finally my chance to try it out! There was a woman on the phone asking to speak to my mom, and my brother explained she wasn't there. She told him, "Oh, okay... well, I just wanted to call and let you know that your daddy has gone to be with Jesus."

My brother casually said, "Okay, I will let her know." Then he hung up the phone.

I thought, *That is strange. Why would someone call to let us know that my step dad went to church? Oh well, that's good, maybe he will finally be nice now.*" After hanging up the phone, I went downstairs as casually as possible, but my brother questioned me immediately to see if I had been listening in on the phone. "No," I lied.

He said "Okay; whatever. Charles died."

Charles? It took me a moment to understand what had just happened. Charles was my dad, my real dad. I did not know him; I had never met him, but now he was dead. I did not know what to say or how to react, so I said nothing at all. I was one year old when my dad left, so I had no memories of him. He had been like an imaginary person to me—one that I dreamed up what he was like because I really had no idea. The man I created in my mind was a figment of my imagination. Although the truth of my dad had the makings of a nice fairy tale, the reality of him was dark and twisted. The truth about him was something I did not find out for many years.

My parents had met each other while serving in children's dorms at the House of Samuel (a home for Indian children) in Tucson Arizona in 1973. They were both Christians. Although dad was much older at 33, and mom 19, they had gotten married quickly. After a few years and the birth of their first child, a girl, they had wanted to continue serving the Lord somewhere besides Arizona. So when a new and unique opportunity came to go to the island of the Dominican Republic and work in a home for troubled teens, they went. Over time they had their first son, Matt. A few years later I was born—a sweet story on the outside.

Sadly, my father had grown up with severe, sexual abuse, something that had left him scarred and damaged. He had many signs of possible mental illness, although never diagnosed, and struggled with the confusion resulting from having been abused so young and for so long.

Now married, he had started having affairs with other men, eventually leading to their divorce. Dad had decided to leave the island and demanded to take one of his children with him. I was too young, and, fearing for my brother being abused as well, mom had only one choice, my older sister. Dad had taken her and returned to the States, and we were left to fend for ourselves. I never saw him again.

Having no memory of my dad and being so young, for me the loss was nothing compared to what it must have been like for my siblings. My brother knew him and didn't understand why he was suddenly gone. My sister had been suddenly separated from the family she knew and taken to a whole new country.

Things had been very hard on the island at times. In the early eighties a recession hit, the economy plummeted, and getting food became scarce. My mom ended up marrying a man from the Dominican Republic in 1980. Sadly, it wasn't long before she realized that she had gone from one abusive relationship to another, a violent one this time. Daily life had been marked by fear and doing whatever we could so that his violence wouldn't be released on all of us. Being a boy, my brother took the brunt of many things, but I had still feared whenever my stepdad came home. Having come from such a different culture and battling his own addictions and inner demons, he was a cold, distant man. I never remember him showing my brother affection, but I do remember him beating him with belts, sticks, and tools—basically anything within reach. I can only remember a few times that he showed me affection, but thankfully I forgot the things he did to hurt me; although my brother remembered them vividly.

When my brother would end up doing something to hurt me like a typical, big brother does (usually while playing), I would do my best to try and cover it up so he wouldn't get into trouble because watching him get punished hurt me more than whatever goofy thing he did. I hated seeing what my stepdad would do to my brother. So naturally my brother and I became very close. We were playmates, and we looked out for each other. We were all we really had. Matt always had a sense of adventure and was great at coming up with crazy ideas that would usually get us into trouble. I would just follow along, trusting him and knowing he would look out for me.

One day my brother wanted a tropical fruit drink that you could get for only a nickel from vendors on the streets. The only problem was that he didn't have money for it. He devised a plan to send me out asking people for money since I was smaller, cuter, and only three years old. Being the only white people in the town, we stood out, and people thought I was extra cute because I was so bald and pale compared to them. So we snuck out a hole in the backyard fence and made our way to find people to give us each a nickel. The plan was genius for a six-year-old boy and would have worked, too, if my parents had not found us before we got to buy the drink. To cover up what we did, I was supposed to hide my nickel, but, since I had no pockets, I decided to hide it in my mouth—not a good place for a coin. Of course, I accidently swallowed it! When questioned by mom on the whereabouts of the money, I merely pointed to my empty but open mouth. After a frantic trip to the doctor for a stunning x-ray of a coin inside my intestines, he assured my mom that what goes in must come out. The nickel was eventually discovered and kept for the sheer humor of the whole thing! Before long my brother found it, took it, and went and bought that tropical drink without me! That was Matt. He could be so determined to do something that nothing could really stop him; whether it was for good or for evil, he couldn't be stopped.

When I was almost five our relatives sent us enough money to get off the island and come back to the United States. For my brother and I it was our first time in America as we were both born in the Dominican Republic and had never left the island. We moved to a small town in Northern California called Grass Valley. I continued shadowing my brother everywhere. I looked up to him, and he was more of a father figure to me than my stepdad. Matt taught me how to play catch and showed me how to ride a bike for the first time without training wheels. He was a true entrepreneur early on and showed me how to make money selling lemonade; doing yard work for the elderly; having a newspaper route; and selling blackberries we picked door to door, anything to support our love of candy or getting the toys we really wanted but couldn't afford. We went on many adventures throughout the small town of Grass Valley, riding bikes and building forts. We invented many games and put on performances for my mom. Through a series of horrible events, my older sister finally made it back into our lives and away from the destructive life of my real father. Then it was like the three amigos, only with a few catfights here and there.

I was six when my first, younger sibling was born. With the arrival of my stepdad's real children, our distant relationship with him became even more distant. So when the death of my real father happened in 1989 when I was ten, the idea of having a dad vanished. I know how hard it was for me to not have a father, but I can only imagine what it was like for my brother. He needed a father. He needed an example of how to be a man, how to live, how to handle himself, how to have relationships, and how to handle the stresses of life.

That night after the phone call about my real dad, I laid in my bed, and I wept. I mourned, but not for the man who had died. After all, how do you mourn someone you never met? Instead, I mourned the death of my dream. My hope was crushed; I had no hope left. Dad had been my last hope. I had wanted him to save me from my painful existence, but now he was gone, and there was nothing left. I was trapped in a home with a stepdad who did not love me, who was abusive to my mom and to us. My mom was overwhelmed, pregnant again, and couldn't see me. Although she loved me, she didn't have time for me amidst all the chaos. We were poor and struggled to get food on the table, let alone the nice clothes it seemed to require to fit in at school. Feeling so alone in a dark and cruel world, despair entered my heart. Now, my daddy was gone forever, and I had never even met him.

Years later I would discover that he had died of AIDS. The consequences of his choices had taken his life. Something in me broke after that. Hardness started to grow and take over my heart and began changing me. I stopped dreaming; I stopped caring.

A few months after my dad died, while I was still ten years old, my best friend stole a joint from her brother and asked me if I wanted to try it. I was curious; I had heard about weed. The mystery was alluring, forbidding, and exciting, so I went for it. One time is all it took. I was hooked. I wasn't hooked on weed after trying it once, but I was hooked on the feeling of being high. I was hooked on the escape, the temporary escape from my reality. I didn't have to pretend I was in a different reality anymore; I really felt like I was. Sadly, it was only an illusion of escape. In truth, it became my master that day, and I was its slave. The chains were shackled onto me right then and there, and there was no escaping it. Thoughts of it came into my mind continually—how to get more, or when I could do it again. I never got as high again as I did that first time, but I pursued that high regardless. It forever changed my life.

Although I was unaware of it at the time, my brother started using drugs as well. He tried to keep it from me so he wouldn't be a bad influence on me. Matt had such an incredible mind; he was intelligent without trying. He could always remember everything! In school, it helped him greatly, but in life it became his nemesis because forgiveness is very difficult when you remember every detail of everything that ever happens. Although he was very intelligent, he lacked basic coping skills for life and for stress. It became a perfect storm for an early discovery of drugs and the temporary escape they offered him. He, too, was quickly hooked. Drugs also brought out the deep-seated anger that was in him, and soon that anger rose to the surface and became very destructive. My mom, being pregnant with her sixth child, having three teenagers, and raising two toddlers, couldn't control him. After a series of bad choices, he was eventually sent to a group home. Although they were only supposed to keep him for 2 weeks while mom had the baby, once he was in the system she couldn't get him out. They kept him in group homes for a year and half. I missed him so much; I felt so alone without him.

Then my sister ran away from home at fifteen, not to be seen or heard from again for years. I was alone and couldn't stand being at home any longer. On top of the craziness and tensions, my mom had her seventh child then separated from my step dad. I started running away from home at twelve years old just after my youngest brother was born. My crazy lifestyle ended up putting me in and out of juvenile hall on a regular basis. After serving time, I would get released to my mom; then I would only stick around for a little while before taking off and ending up back on the streets. This became the pattern for my life, and the cycle would begin again and again. My love of weed grew deeper, and I started smoking it every day, all throughout the day. I thought, somehow, I was smarter when I smoked it, more intuitive. I thought I enjoyed things like movies and food more when I used it. Before long, I couldn't really enjoy things without it. I didn't even feel "normal" until I smoked it. Soon it wasn't enough anymore. I started dabbling with other drugs by the time I was twelve.

Acid, mushrooms, pills, and meth were my next experiments. The thought of trying something new was exciting and enticing, so I was willing to try anything. I didn't even like crystal meth much at first; yet, somehow, I always went back to it. It was cheap, easy to get, and a lot of people I knew were doing it, it came naturally. At first, I would just stay up for a night or two on it and tweak out, then not use it again for a while. Eventually, I hated the feeling of "coming down" so much that I would use it again to get back "up". While I was on it, I was numb, with no emotions, and no pain. When it wore off, the emotions came one hundred times stronger, and I couldn't handle it. Because of the people I was choosing to be around and the lifestyle I was living, I kept putting myself in situations where I would get hurt physically and emotionally. I was assaulted, robbed, rejected many times, and even raped. Because all of these things would create more and more pain within me, I would have to numb myself more. Continually putting myself in dangerous places meant it was not safe to sleep. When I would sleep, I was haunted by dark, terrifying nightmares, so I decided not to sleep at all. I would use meth and stay up for many nights until my body would shut itself down and collapse. Days later I would wake up not remembering anything. The hallucinations would increase the longer I was up, and I lived in a state of constant paranoia. At night I could see the shadows coming to life and people in trees watching me. During the day, I feared being seen by the police, so I stayed indoors. In my pursuit to be high, I reached an incredible low. Meth was killing me. I was shriveling away. My teeth were rotting out of my mouth. Looking like death, I even started to long for it. I was a prisoner of my own doing, not sure how to escape my own, personal hell.

As I looked into the mirror that day in 1994 at the age of fifteen, I saw myself as I really was...on the verge of death; yet death seemed to be the only way to escape this nightmare. I hoped that somehow there would be another way. I just wanted to be happy. *Will I ever be happy?* I wanted to dream again, to hope that there could be a future for me, but I was so empty. *There has to be more than this!* I often thought to myself. The shame tormented me. I could see it in my eyes. *I have to get away from meth; I am too young to die like this.* I knew that I could not escape this cruel, slave master on my own. I knew it would take being forced away from it. Well aware of my own weaknesses, I concluded that I would have to be a prisoner for me to escape this self-made prison. So that day after seeing my true reflection in the mirror, I turned myself in to the police and willingly went to juvenile hall. It was the only place that I knew of where I was safe from meth; it couldn't get me there. I could eat and sleep, get my mind back, and put some meat on my bones. I realized then that I needed to lose my freedom just so I could get it back again.

Chapter 3
A Kidnapper's Mission

"Defend the poor and fatherless; do justice to the afflicted and needy.
Deliver the poor and needy; free them from the hand of the wicked."
Psalm 82:3-4 (NKJV)

February 1995, Redding, California

HOW DID I GET HERE? I have been kidnapped, alone in a truck with a meth addict! Where is he taking me? What will he do to me when we get there? He is going to murder me! I have to get out of this truck! The door won't open; it won't unlock! What am I going to do?

This guy is crazy! Why is he talking to his truck? Who is he talking to?

Why did he take me? I don't know where we are. I don't know my way around this city. I don't know what to do!

Why does he keep talking to the dashboard? I don't hear anyone else, but he is having a conversation with his truck! Dear God, this lunatic is going to murder me!

Why did I leave the group home? I was safe there; just a few short days ago, I was there, safe...or was it a week ago? Again, I had lost all sense of time. I had used again. Why did I use again?

I should have stayed at the group home; the people who ran it were nice. I could have finished high school; I could have been safe!

I had run from the group home, not because it was a bad place but because I didn't want to be controlled. I didn't want anyone telling me what I had to do. I wanted to be in control! *Are you in control now, Joy,... trapped in a truck with some lunatic who kidnapped you from a party?* I argued with myself. Again, in my pursuit of freedom, I had become a prisoner.

My abductor drove off the main road and into the woods. *This is it; this is where he will rape and kill me.* He pulled the truck over but kept it running. My heart was racing; every muscle in my body was tense. I had no intention of going down without a fight. I knew I would only have one chance, so I waited for the right moment.

He pulled out a glass pipe and started to smoke from it while he talked to me. He explained that he knew I was under eighteen even though I had lied to the people at the party. He said he was on a mission that he had a special purpose. He was supposed to "save children." He knew I was a child who needed to be saved. *How did he know?* "They" had told him. He promised that he would not hurt me in any way and that he would save me. That is why he took me from the party; it was not safe there. He handed me the pipe. I was shaking as I held the pipe in my hand. My mind raced. *Should I smoke this? What if it is laced? Well, he just smoked it so it can't be laced.* I rationalized to myself. *It will help me not sleep. I have to stay awake.* Convincing myself it would somehow help my crazy situation, I smoked the meth. He assured me that everything was going to be fine; we had to follow the signs. There was a secret network of people helping him on his mission. I would be safe; I needed to trust him.

He told me about his daughter; she was also fifteen years old. He said he was unable to be there for her, to help her, but he would help me—it was his mission. He asked me, "Is there anywhere you would want to go, if I could get you there?" Stunned, I thought to myself. *"Where would I go? Could he be serious? I am on the run...again. This time I am in a city I have never been to before, Redding, with active warrants for my arrest...again!"*

I told him, "I know that I can't go to Grass Valley. The cops all know me there, and I would get arrested in no time!" My mind raced, thinking of something, anything, anywhere I could possibly go. A small glimmer of hope flashed quickly in my mind. A completely crazy thought. *No, it's impossible.* I thought to myself. *Besides, I can't trust him...can I?* I thought about my last encounter with my stepdad. Before the group home, he had come to see me while I was in juvenile hall. It had been a long time since we had last been in contact. He had left and divorced my mom. He told me about how he had moved to Florida, how it was much better out there with multiple job opportunities. He said I should come see him out there sometime. *Well, this was sometime; could it be possible?* I knew it was crazy, but, having no other options, I finally spoke and said, "Florida. I would go to Florida. If I could go anywhere, that's where it would be because there is nothing left for me here in California."

He agreed; it was settled. His "mission" was to get me to Florida. He communicated with his truck by leaning in toward the dashboard and talking in a low quiet voice. Once he finished updating "them" on the plan, he turned the music up. He played the same tape over and over again...the "Free Falling" album by Tom Petty. That music always played unless "they" were talking to him or when he was talking to the secret network of people I could not hear. I was stunned. *What sort of weird twilight zone was I in now?* A crazy meth addict had abducted me from a party that I had found after I had broken out of a lockdown group home. I was in Redding, California, somewhere I had never been. I had never met this guy before, but he was now suddenly on a "mission" to get me across the U.S. to Florida.

How did I get here? Do I really trust this guy? Do I have a choice? I do not know where I am, and I do not know where I would go if I did decide to run! He says he won't hurt me; so for now, I will trust him. I do not have any other choice. There is nowhere left for me to go; all I have is a small glimmer of hope that somehow, some way, this crazy guy is going to get me out of California. Could this really be happening?

Reality and insanity had merged into a dark underworld where fear was now my only companion. Suddenly, and out of nowhere, I was under the control and presumed care of someone who was now on a "mission" from the voices in his head to save me! I refused to let my guard down for a moment, knowing how quickly things could change, but I held on to the only hope that I had...that this crazy stranger would actually do what he said and help me.

The Florida mission was set, and my abductor/rescuer, who I found out was named Craig, decided he would drive me to the Greyhound bus station in Sacramento, purchase a bus ticket to Florida, and off I would go. I called my stepdad, and, surprisingly, he said I could stay with him and that he wouldn't tell anyone. Craig drove me to Grass Valley so I could see my sister who had been gone for years; it was a great risk since it was my hometown and all the cops knew me. We made it short and sweet; I saw her and was able to say goodbye, then left town right away. He had to drive back up to Redding to pick up a check so he would have the money to send me on my way. The entire time I was there, I was terrified that we would get stopped and I would never make it to Sacramento, but that, too, was a short trip into town then out again. By the time we arrived in Sacramento, it was dark, and the station was closed. Outside the entrance was a group of guys hanging out in the shadows. My heart was racing. *Will he leave me here?* He took a good look and said, "This isn't safe; I can't leave you here. Let's go to L.A., and I can put you on a train instead." I was so relieved. He really did want me safe, so I finally let my guard down completely; then everything went black.

My eyes opened, and everything was spinning. I awoke to the force of flying forward and my heading hitting the dashboard. The intense pain brought me back to reality. I passed out. After being up for three days (or was it four?) my body shut down, and I fell asleep. We had been driving for so long, the road was dark, and there were very few cars out at that time of night. In my state of paranoia, I watched every set of headlights to make sure they weren't cops. I remembered a small, gray truck that passed us earlier; they were in a hurry and passed us quickly. It stood out to me because it looked exactly like the truck I was in, a small two-door, gray, Toyota truck. The road was so long, so boring, so dark, and there were very few cars to watch. I fell asleep and forgot all about that other truck. Now there it was, in front of us. The front end was smashed in like a can; the hood rested on the roof of the truck, and I could see small flames flickering in the engine. There was a man standing outside the driver's side door; he was holding his head with both of his hands. *He must not see the fire.* I thought to myself. Then I saw someone moving in the truck! Craig told me to help them; "Get out quick!"

I ran over to the truck just as a woman was stumbling out. I could hear a little child crying in the truck. The woman was dazed and disoriented, no doubt in shock at what had happened. I could hear Craig in the background yelling for me to hurry. I grabbed the child, a little girl, and helped her out of the truck. She was small, maybe around five years old; she was crying, scared, and confused. Craig kept yelling, "Hurry! Bring her over here!" I carried her over to our truck while the woman went around to check on the man. I kept telling the little girl, "It will be okay." *Will it?* I managed to get her to the seat of the truck where I had been sitting. Suddenly, before I even realized it, Craig floored it, and the truck took off!

He drove off so fast, I flew back and hit the ground before I even realized what had happened. Then it hit me. *He took her!* He kidnapped the little girl the way he had taken me from the party! I stood up, watching in complete shock as the truck drove away with gravel flying everywhere. I turned to look at the poor couple who had survived a car accident only to watch their little girl get abducted right before their very eyes. Before my eyes could focus on where they were, a bright light flashed before me, followed by the sound of screeching brakes so loud that I could feel it throughout my whole body. An oncoming car crashed into the wrecked truck in the middle of the road, smashing it like an aluminum can. The sound of crushing metal and breaking glass filled the once quiet night. Pieces of shattered glass whizzed by me like bullets as I stood there six feet from the collision. I looked down at my body expecting to see blood from the glass or sharp pieces of metal that must have hit me...but nothing! It was as if something had protected me, like I was somehow in a bubble protected by the flying projectiles that flew at me. *How is this even possible?* Then I saw Craig driving back with his hazard lights on, and he parked behind the wreck, trying to warn any other oncoming cars. He had seen the car coming and reacted in time to get out of the way with the girl. My heart was racing; I was trembling. *Did this really just happen?* I was relieved that the girl had not been kidnapped but was only in shock from what had just taken place.

This young family had been on their way to Disneyland. To save time, they had decided to drive through the night. They were driving at full speed when they had hit a cow in the middle of the road! A cow! I never could have imagined that the damage done to that truck was from hitting a cow! Other cars stopped to help; eventually the highway patrol and ambulance arrived. We gave our stories to the officers. The looks of suspicion were all over their faces, but they took down our accounts and let us go. I pretended to be Craig's daughter and even used her name, Chelsea. Before I knew it, we were driving again. My mind was racing as I looked in the side view mirror just waiting for the red and blue flashing lights to be behind us, but they never did.

Our journey continued to L.A.; I had never been there before. The sun was rising when we drove into the city. I had never seen a city so big! Before I knew it, we made it to the train station. It was a beautiful place with amazing architecture and detail, so full of people moving about it! It looked to me like thousands of bees moving around a hive. There were so many people everywhere, people who all knew where they were going, knew what they were doing. *Where am I going? What am I doing? What lay ahead of me?* I was taking a train into the great unknown. *Would it be safe? Would I find my "home", a place where I belonged?*

I pushed my doubts and fears aside; they really didn't matter. What awaited me on the other side of the U.S. didn't matter. I had to get out of California. Craig purchased me a train ticket under his daughter's name, gave me a few dollars for food, then waited with me until it was time to board. When the time came, I boarded the train after saying a very awkward goodbye and a thank you to this very unusual man. I had a strange relationship with this man who snatched me from all that I knew in California and changed the course of my life. True to his word, he never hurt me in any way. Once I was safely on the train, he left the station, and I never saw him again. His "mission" was accomplished; he had indeed saved me, a child, from danger and had successfully sent me on my way to the only place I could think of to go—Florida.

Chapter 4
Homeless and Alone

"The way of the wicked is like darkness,
they do not know what makes them stumble."
Proverbs 4:19 (NKJV)

March 1995, Panama City Beach, Florida

HOW DID I GET HERE? Alone, homeless on the streets, at sixteen years old. I had warrants for my arrest in California for running from a lockdown group home. I did not have any friends in the entire state of Florida; I had never been there before. This was on the other side of the country! The only person I did know had no compassion for what would or could happen to me; he only cared about his own inconveniences. That was what I was; that is all I was, an inconvenience. Did he have any idea what I had gone through to get here? Of course not, this wasn't what was supposed to happen. I knew I couldn't trust my stepdad, but I had no choice.

At first all seemed good; he welcomed me into his apartment in Panama City Beach, Florida, after picking me up from the train stop. There was no station near where he lived, so I was dropped off in what seemed like the middle of nowhere, but he was there to get me, just like he said. My step dad said he wanted to help me, that he cared about me, and he "always saw me as a daughter." *A daughter...strange, he had never treated me like one.* I could count on one hand the few times he hugged me as a child. He was a cold and distant overseer, a demanding, violent, and controlling ruler of the house. He was one who could not stand happiness or holidays unless he was drunk. Every holiday had been the opportunity to flex his control over all and crush down any chance of a peaceful, enjoyable time together. I had grown to dread holidays and birthdays. Those special occasions and the expectation to be "kind" had been his time to be cruel, like a child who has been told he has to be nice he spitefully does the opposite. Although a man of inner chaos, he had demanded outer order...obsessively. He embodied obsessive compulsive disorder before it had a definition. Every pencil, every paper, and every object had to be in line or the inner chaos came out on us all. He had demanded perfection yet had given nothing in return to show any approval or affection to his "step" children. I had known I could never measure up, nor be perfect, so I knew he would never love me nor accept me. I only knew my fear of him. However, now he was my last hope, so I had to trust him.

I did not expect him to be my "dad". That was a word as foreign to me as "home". So when he said "like a daughter", my stomach knotted up knowing something was strange about it, something unnatural. Clearly he had had a few drinks before he said it, so that explained the expressed emotion and empty promises. He could not possibly see me as a daughter. I chose to trust him anyway, not because he was trustworthy but from complete and total desperation. That trust gave me a few weeks; that was it.

The inconvenience of sharing a room with his "daughter" was greater than the promise to help her. After all, he had a girlfriend now. How could that work? He shared the two bedroom apartment with another couple, and their brother was "renting" the couch in the living room. Where did that leave this young girl with no money? Certainly not in the same room with him. So, she must go, too great of an inconvenience. Just like that, I was homeless again.

This time it was much different though; in Grass Valley, I knew people. In my own town I always knew of somewhere I could lay my head, somewhere I could hang out until daylight. Now I was completely alone with no one to call. I still had to avoid the police and had nothing but a backpack with a few clothes. The only thing going for me was the job I had just gotten at a t-shirt shop on the beach. I just needed to work and save some money, then I would be okay. I had to be okay. The weather was warm, so I could sleep anywhere and be okay; or so I hoped.

I went to work my first day, my first real job. I had just turned sixteen years old a few days before. The manager was showing me around and what to do. He took me to the back room and started telling me something. His Arab accent was so strong I had a hard time understanding what he was saying. *Did he really say what I think he said? Could this really be happening?* Yes, I could see the way he was looking at me. He reached his hand behind me to pull me closer to him. I stepped back and pushed him away. He said if I didn't do this with him then I didn't have a job. I quickly ran out of there with tears in my eyes knowing that he had hired me for one purpose and one purpose only. This was not the first time a man saw only what he could take from me. He did not see me. I was merely an object, a thing to take control of for his own lust, not a person of value or importance, a thing to use and throw away. The pain of past sexual assaults was still fresh on my mind and I vowed to never allow it to happen again. So just like that, I lost my job before it even started.

I truly was alone in this life and only had myself to trust. Yet even that trust was easily broken. I was quick to do things that would harm myself if only for the promise of temporary relief from pain. An illusion of happiness was all I could obtain, so I would search for it until I found it. That was exactly what I did on the streets of Panama City Beach, Florida. I found a party, got wasted, and pretended like everything was great. It was spring break; there were parties everywhere. Turns out I had landed in the spring break party capital of the world! It was a beautiful place with sugar white sand beaches, aquamarine waters, and miles of hotels full of college kids on vacation living it up. They were all kids who had families back home that cared about them, they were just here to have fun. Afterwards, they would return to their real lives where they had a future ahead of them, a good education, and a future career with money and security. Me? What future did I have? What security? What way to make money? What career? My reality was such a contrast compared to these kids, so I just pretended to be one of them. Just for fun, I invented a college I was from and fabricated a different name. Only, it wasn't fun. I knew the truth. The truth was I had no hope; I had no future.

I ended up finding a party that was at a house not a hotel. This one was different, not a bunch of spring breakers but locals, people who actually lived in that town. I ended up talking with a young couple for a while. They were a really cute couple from Tennessee; I loved their Southern accent! They had been living there for about a year. Her name was Melissa, but she went by Missy. His name was Nick. I opened up to them about my situation, not everything, of course, but the main part about my stepdad kicking me out and how I was in a new state where I did not know anyone. As fate would have it, they were looking for a roommate!

They had an apartment on the beach and needed someone to rent a bedroom to offset the cost. They offered it to me! I did not know how I would afford it, but I did not care. I would figure out a way. I just needed to get off the streets, and I did. A real place to live...a bedroom, a shower. It even had a bed, a real place! Now I only had to figure out how to keep it. Thankfully, the apartment was just off the main strip, so there were plenty of places to walk. There were many restaurants, but, in order to wait tables and serve alcohol, you had to be eighteen years old. I looked eighteen. I had that going for me, so I applied at many places. Finally, one called me back. I lied about my age, I said I was nineteen. It worked! They hired me! When they asked for my identification, I told them that my purse had been stolen and I was waiting for my mom to mail my birth certificate from California so I could get a new one. It was a believable story. They could tell I was not from around there and had a different accent, so they let me work. I was determined to be the best employee they had. I never wanted them to question me or have a reason to get rid of me, so I worked extra shifts. I went above and beyond my job description. I was reliable, and I was always on time.

Unfortunately, when tax time would roll around, they would go into my file and see there was no driver's license or identification on file for me. When they asked for it, I always told them I would bring it "tomorrow." When tomorrow finally came, I had to go and look for another job.

If only I was eighteen. If only I did not have warrants for my arrest. If only my past would quit haunting me! I was free from the grips of meth, finally, (only because there was no meth around there) but the grips of my past I could not shake. I wanted to finish high school, but fear of arrest was always there. I had to face my warrants. I did not want to run forever. I was tired of the fear that would paralyze me if I saw a policeman. I wanted to do good. Although I wanted to make it somehow despite all I had been through, it was always there in the back of my mind, holding me back from moving forward. I wanted to dream of having a real future again. I decided it was time; I had to go back to California. I had to face my past, or there was no way I could have a future.

Chapter 5
Escape From Rage

"Make no friendship with a angry man,
and with a furious man do not go."
Proverbs 22:24 (NKJV)

July 1997, Panama City Beach, FL

HOW DID I GET HERE? He is going to murder me; he is crazy enough to do it. This is it; this is really it. This is how I will die, murdered by the man I love. He is really going to murder me. He said he will take me to some swamp and that they won't be able to find me; there won't be pieces of me left to find.

My mind was racing trying to think of the remote place he would take me. *He grew up here; he knew just where to go. How would I get away? He is stronger and faster; I don't stand a chance!* The truck was driving too fast for me to jump out and he continued to drive erratically while cursing threats under his breath. *How can I get away from him?*

I thought about the criminal cases I was learning about in college. I had started taking pre-legal classes; I wanted to become a lawyer since I already knew so much about the legal system. After having my warrants forgiven by the judge in California, my record sealed, and even being emancipated, I had returned to Florida and gotten my GED, then also started college. It was just before then that I had met my boyfriend Damon. He had even encouraged me to sign up for the college classes.

Damon and I had met at a mutual friend's house, we immediately started talking and things moved quickly, too quickly. We were inseprable. I thought he was my soul mate, we were madly in love and decided to move in together after dating for only a few months. His dark and violent side only started to show its face after we were living together. It started small, a push during an argument. He felt so terrible about it and begged me to forgive him. Then it progressed to a slap in the face. Again, he begged and pleaded and swore it would never happen again, so I forgave him. Once he knew that he could beg and plead for me to forgive him, he knew I was his and it didn't matter what he did I would always come back. Now it was to the point that he said he would kill me.

It was in my Criminal Procedures class in college that I learned about a case that would have been unsolvable and unprovable had it not been for the victim scratching the killer and leaving his DNA under her fingernails. In that moment after he threatened to murder me, I was determined to scratch, to leave some evidence of the one who killed me, if they ever found me.

We had been driving somewhere when we had an argument. It escalated quickly and had turned to screaming. He back-handed me in the face so I yelled that I was going to leave him. That's when he told me he would kill me. He sped up, driving erratically in a different direction than we were going. *He's really going to do it this time! Who would report me missing? Will they ever find me?* I had no friends or family because he had isolated me from everyone. I belonged to him and him only. He said he loved me; I fell for it. I fell for him. I finally thought I could be happy, that I could be loved. I was wrong again! Now, in a fit of rage, he would murder me and leave my body to be devoured by alligators in some Florida swamp. My thoughts were racing. *No, it can't end like this. I cannot give up, I have to fight. You are a fighter, but I am no match for him. RUN! You have to run, Joy!* I finally convinced myself.

The fear was paralyzing. I was trembling, but I knew I had to get away before we got to a remote place. The truck was driving too fast for me to jump out. *You can't let him get you out of town. You have to get out of this truck! I have to wait for the perfect moment.* Finally, the truck slowed down at a stop light. *Now!* I jumped out of the truck once it slowed down, then fell to the ground. I picked myself up off the ground as fast as I could and ran. The hot, humid air clung to me like a heavy blanket. I could barely breathe, but I ran, and I ran. I ran toward the town, through streets, weaving my way through them hoping he couldn't work his truck around fast enough. I knew I needed to find a public place, somewhere that people could help me. I saw a clothing store. I knew he had to be turned around by now and close, so I ran inside.

Hide! You have to hide! I told myself. Running into the store terrified, I found the dressing rooms and hid. I had to be still. I had to slow down my breathing. I heard a jingling as the front doors to the store opened. *Please, God, don't let it be him!* "Hey, bro; what's up, man?" I recognized his voice. Then I realized it was a greeting of recognition.

"Oh, I am doing good. What are you up to?" the worker answered. Of all the places I had run to, I found one that was employed by his friends.

"Oh, not much. Hey, I am looking for my girlfriend. I saw her come in here. Skinny blonde, you see her?"

"Oh yeah, she is in that dressing room right there," he replied casually then walked away, a good time to take a smoke break.

My boyfriend walked up to the dressing room, ripped the curtain open, came in, shut it behind him, then grabbed me by my hair, and whispered into my ear. "This is your chance to live. Just do what I say and everything will be fine. We can pretend that nothing ever happened today and go back to how things were. I love you; and I can't live without you, and you won't live without me." Simple really. I was trapped. There was no use in leaving him; he would find me.

My chance to live meant that once again I had become a slave. There was no escape, nowhere to run; he would always find me. I belonged to him; he was my master now, my cruel master. I went back with him. What else could I do?

As I continued pursuing my pre-legal degree, I took more and more classes that made my living situation seem very ironic. My Family Law class had weeks on domestic violence alone. I would endure abuse all week, then study about it at night in my class! I learned about the statistics of domestic abuse, and sadly the many that ended in murder. There were lessons on the procedures of anger management for people arrested for domestic violence and even how the majority of police calls are over domestic disputes. As I would try to tell myself the lies: "He will change because loves me". My classes would show me overwhelming evidence to the contrary. I knew deep down that I had to escape him. How could I get away? Every time I did leave him, he would always find me and somehow get me to come back. I had gotten to the point that I believed I deserved what he was doing to me; I didn't know any differently. This was the only love I knew; yet somehow, it was killing me. I even fantasized about killing him and being free once and for all, but I knew of many cases where the woman still spent life in prison. That was not the freedom I wanted, free from him but not free to live. I wanted to be loved so desperately.

In between the abuse, he would show me love—just enough so I wanted to stay with him. He would show so much remorse after one of his episodes that I would easily forgive him when he hurt me. He never made me feel valued or like I could deserve more than what he gave me. In fact, it was always my fault—if only I was different, then he wouldn't hit me. If I would have just done what he said, or maybe if I reacted differently. If I could just be better. I knew I could never measure up, so the abuse would never stop. Yet, I continued to blame myself; I even made excuses for him. I continued to excuse reality, until one day reality slammed my face in the door, literally.

One night I woke up lying on the ground. He was weeping over my body. He thought he had killed me. The last thing I remembered was him strangling me—the look of madness in his eyes, the darkness looking into me and through me as he squeezed the life out of me. *Why now? Why does he cry now?* In the heat of the moment, he thought he had done it; he thought I was dead. Did he cry over the loss of my life? No...but the loss of his. I am sure the tears were for the thought of spending life in prison, not for the life he took from me.

He saw me move, then grabbed me up, and hugged me, weeping. "I will never do this again; I promise you." *Promise? What does that even mean?* I knew that this was it. He would eventually kill me, or I would have to kill him. Just the week before, he had slammed my face in the door; the bruises were still fresh. Earlier that day he had thrown my small puppy across the room. My sweet, little, Pomeranian puppy, my tiny little thing. That little dog looked at me with such love, such unconditional love. How could anyone hurt this tiny, little thing? In my heart I knew that if he could hurt this tiny, little puppy, then he could hurt a child, my child. I knew that I could not risk having this man's child. He would do to him what he had done to me. My life was not valuable enough to matter, but the thought of a child's life did matter. I had to leave, or die trying, but I had to leave.

I was secretly saving money, knowing the day would come when I had to run. In the fall of 1998 I was in the middle of a college semester, one and a half years into a two year Associate of Science degree. I knew that if I left, he would just find me at the school. He knew the location and times of my classes, so I made the decision to walk away from it, all of it. The degree would not help me if I was dead; if I didn't leave soon I would not survive. He would not suspect me leaving at this time, so his grip on me wouldn't be as tight. I also knew that in order to get away I had to leave behind my things, all my furniture, belongings, everything. So I could have a head start, it had to be at a time he didn't think I would go and during a time of day he wouldn't know I was gone for a while.

One day after he left for work, I was supposed to go to my job, but instead I left him. I took very few things with me, and I left. I had people who helped me hide for a while until I could figure out where to go. I had to leave Panama City Beach, go somewhere new. I decided to go to Orlando; a friend I knew had moved there and offered to let me stay with her for a while. Leaving would have been easier, if not for what I was leaving behind, my dog. I couldn't take him where I was going, so I had no choice but to leave him, too.

The day I had gotten my puppy, I had no intention of getting a dog. I saw a pet store as I was driving by and decided to stop in just for fun, just to kill some time. When I walked into the store, I saw a wall full of cages. There were all sorts of barking and meowing animals in the cages. Then I noticed one cage that had no movement, just a ball of fur in the corner. Curious, I went closer just to see what it was. The little ball of fur started moving. It got up on his little feet, then walked toward me. He looked like a little baby Ewok from the movie *Star Wars*. He had tan fur on his belly and black fur everywhere else. I don't think I had ever seen anything so cute. Looking so sad, he came right up to the cage like he wanted to touch me. I moved my face toward him, and he licked me. He looked like he was crying. I didn't know if dogs cried or not as I had never had one; I always wanted one as a kid but never owned one. It turned out that they had just sold his sister that day, so I imagine he really was sad. Once he licked me, I knew it was all over; this baby was mine. I asked how much and brought him home. My boyfriend wasn't thrilled, but he, too, couldn't resist this dog's cuteness. Sadly after only a few days, the dog became very sick. I took him to the vet, and he determined that he had a parasite and sent me home with medicine. He only got worse. He was lying on my chest as I was on the couch when he started to have seizures. I was so scared for him! The vet was closed due to a holiday, so I had to wait. Once the doctor returned, he told me he not only had a parasite but also had parvo; it didn't look good. Parvo is so deadly to animals that few survive it. The vet kept him for a few days and gave him a blood transfusion; somehow he survived! This dog had fought some incredible odds and survived! That puppy loved me so much; he went everywhere with me. I could hide him in my shirt or in a bag, so he even went to the movies or grocery stores. I loved him; he always made me smile. I knew he loved me, too.

I thought about the time when I was on the ground as my boyfriend was hitting me in a fit of rage. My arms were covering my face as he was hitting the back of my head, then hitting my torso over and over. I curled up in a ball on the ground when that little pup came up to me and climbed onto my face. It was like he was trying to protect me. In a way he did; it did make my abuser stop and walk away. I feared for that little dog from then on. *Would he kill him just to get back at me?* This dog had already been through so much, yet survived, just like me. I felt connected to him somehow.

After reminiscing for a few weeks, I decided that I could not leave that dog. I had to take the risk of returning for this little thing that was willing to risk himself for me. Choosing a time of day when my boyfriend should have been at work, I drove back to Panama City. In hindsight I should have run into the house, grabbed the dog, and run out. However, when I thought about the other things I was leaving, I decided to grab a few of them, a big mistake. I walked out the bedroom, and there he was, standing there. My greatest fear came true. He was shocked to see me in the house; I was shocked to see him. He should have been at work, but he had come home for something.

My heart was pounding so hard I could feel it in my throat; my hands were trembling. *What would he do? Would he go into a rage?* Crying and begging me to come back, he promised he would never hit me again. He started punching himself in the face and saying he would only hit himself and wouldn't hit me ever again. Just then our roommate walked in; he saw what was happening and had a look of panic on his face. He didn't know what to do. He didn't know what this guy would do. I think he had always reasoned away what was happening when we would fight. Maybe he told himself he wasn't really hurting me. Maybe he didn't care, or maybe he felt helpless to do anything about it. Maybe the bond of his friendship was too great to do something about him hurting his girlfriend. He had no loyalty to me but much loyalty to his childhood friend. There was no denying the insanity at this point. It was right before him. He sat down at the table and tried reasoning with him.

Reasoning? Really? In a hysterical rage, my boyfriend grabbed the block of knives on the counter and threw them to the ground. He pulled out a large knife from the case and started stabbing the carpet. I made eye contact with our roommate, and we spoke without saying a word. *We are going to die; he will kill us both.*

I don't know how long we were there waiting to die; time is a strange thing. I just kept thinking that I didn't want to die, but there was nothing I could do or say to calm him at this point. Even the roommate became quiet knowing that any little thing could send him over the edge and we could be gone in a moment. Before I realized it, my boyfriend had gone into the other room. He was crying again and hitting his head against the wall over and over again. I looked at our roommate, and he mouthed "Run!" to me. He realized then what he had reasoned away all those months living in that house. I grabbed the puppy and ran as fast as I could out the door. As I ran, I expected him to catch me by grabbing my hair at any moment and dragging me back, but instead I made it to my car and jumped in. My hands were trembling, shaking uncontrollably. I was fumbling with my keys trying to find the right one. Like in a horror movie, I expected him to come and break my window and drag me back into the house. Instead, I found the right key, started the car, and peeled out of there as fast as my little car could go. I made it; I could not believe I made it out of there! I left behind most of my clothes, my furniture, my possessions, things I could not replace and things I could, but I made it out of there with my life and with the life of the one thing in Florida that really loved me, my little Pomeranian puppy.

Chapter 6
Prisoner of Affliction

"Before I was afflicted I went astray, but now I keep your word."
Psalm 119:67 (NKJV)

January 1999, West Palm Beach, FL

HOW DID I GET HERE? I am alone and afraid in a hospital bed. What will the doctors say? What is wrong with me? The pain in my lower abdomen was a constant reminder that something was very wrong. It was like an alarm going off in my mind screaming for me to get help. So here I was trying to get help. Can they even help me? Several days had passed without answers. What was wrong? At first, they thought it might have been appendicitis, but once that was ruled out many tests followed; yet, no answers. I felt so alone. I was alone; there was no one I could call to come and be with me. Because my crazy ex-boyfriend kept coming after me, I had moved over and over again. Did I move nine or ten times? I had lost count.

I had finally settled down and gotten an apartment in West Palm Beach, Florida. It made me feel so free to have my own place and to finally be able to start a new life! I loved my apartment, my first apartment that was all mine. I didn't even have furniture yet; I was sleeping on an air mattress, so the two bedroom apartment was very empty.

I had only been there a few weeks when one day a sharp pain started in my side. Choosing to ignore it, I assumed it was probably some sort of female issue that would pass. It did not. It got worse by the day until someone mentioned to me that it could be serious and that I really needed to go to a doctor. Fearing an appendicitis, I was checked into the hospital, but they soon realized that was not it. I stayed there uncertain of what was wrong, wondering what would happen, waiting for test results, and waiting for answers. I tried not to be scared, but my own dark thoughts betrayed and haunted me. *This is it. This is it, Joy. They will come in and tell you that you have AIDS; you will die, all alone, just like your father.*

My father. I thought of the man who gave me life, the man who should have been there for me but never was. The way he lived his life was what ended up taking it from him. *Was that what would happen to me?* Thoughts of cancer or some other unusual illness followed. The pain wouldn't stop; it kept screaming fear to me. *I am only nineteen years old. What could be wrong with me?* I called my mom to tell her what was going on. *What could she possibly do on the other side of the country?* My poor, little dog had been left alone in my apartment. I ended up calling the apartment manager and begging her to let him out. She took him home with her and was caring for him. Desperate to talk to someone who cared about me, I even called my ex-boyfriend. He seemed like he did care but then demanded to know where I was, so I hung up. I had come too far to go back now. So, I waited, waited...alone. The doctor finally came in only to tell me that they did not know what was wrong. All the tests had come back fine, but something was wrong. The doctor wanted to do exploratory surgery into my abdomen to see what they could find. It really was my only option to figure out what was wrong, so I agreed.

When I woke up from surgery, the pain was excruciating! I had never experienced anything like it. The following morning the doctors came in to talk with me. They told me that they had found out what was wrong. They seemed pleased to have discovered it but not sure how to explain it to me. "You have what's called endometriosis. It is a disease on the female organs where uterine tissue grows outside the uterus. You have a severe case, and we found lesions throughout your abdomen, on your uterus, bladder, and your bowel. We lasered the lesions, but there is no cure for this disease."

I had never even heard of this before. *What do you mean I have a disease?* I thought to myself, unable to speak. I can only imagine what my expression was; I was shocked, scared, and very confused. They seemed so professional, so clinical, and so by the book. There was no compassion. He said things about follow up and something about drug treatments then immediately talked about discharging me from the hospital. Leaving seemed impossible because I was still so groggy and medicated from the surgery and the pain was so intense. I thought about trying to drive myself home in this condition. "Is there any way I can stay here a little longer? I don't have anyone who can come and pick me up, and I am in too much pain to drive home," tears filled my eyes as I explained. One of the staff there with the doctor turned and looked at me. I will never forget her response to my plea. She said, "Do you know how high of a bill you have accumulated? We need to get you out of here." Just like that they were finished with me; their job was done. What happened to me was no longer their concern. I had never been so afraid to drive before. The pain was so strong that it was hard to walk. A nurse wheeled me out in a wheelchair. Once we got to the entrance of the hospital, I walked around trying to find my car.

I didn't even know where it was. She had compassion on me and helped me look. Finally, we found it. I asked her for directions because I didn't even know how to get home from there. Thankfully she wrote down how to get to the nearest pharmacy and how to get to my side of town. As I got behind the wheel of my car, with the door shut, the loneliness and pain swallowed me up, and I just cried. Completely overwhelmed and afraid, I was terrified. *How could I possibly drive right now?* It had only been twelve hours since my abdominal surgery, and there I was about to drive a car! Once again, I had no choice; I had to do it. Every bump in the road was horrible, the pain overwhelming. Nauseous, dizzy, and drugged from all the meds and the anesthesia, driving felt like a strange video game I was in not reality. Then somehow after making it to the pharmacy, I was left only to realize that I did not have enough money to pay for the prescription. Tears flowed uncontrollably. I just wanted to get the pain pills and get home; I desperately needed to lie down. Frantically digging through my purse searching for money, I was fortunate enough to find enough loose change at the bottom. Somehow, it was exactly enough! Relieved, I got the pain pills and headed for my apartment.

It was so empty there. I hadn't noticed it as much before, but it was so empty; I was alone. Not even my little dog was there to greet me, to make me feel like somebody there loved me and missed me while I was gone. Walking into the bedroom, I took one look at the air mattress I had been sleeping on and knew it wouldn't work. I could not lie in any position to help the pain stop. Once I was lying down I could not get up. I had to roll to get out of it. It was hard to get in and out of the bed when I was normal, but, after abdominal surgery, it seemed impossible! Trying to use my abdominal muscles was torture; the pain was unbearable. I felt like I just could not do it anymore. Weak and in tremendous pain, the overwhelming feeling that I could not go on any longer washed over me. I sat there crying for a long time.

Grabbing the pain pills, I thought of my only way out of this one. *This was it. I was going to end it now; I am finished.* I decided I should pray before I took that whole bottle of pills. *What if there is a God? I am sure he hates me, but I had better make some effort if I am about to face him.* So, I said a simple prayer, the first I had prayed in many years.

"God, I am sorry. I do not want to die right now, but I do not want to live either. I am going to take these pills. If I wake up, great; if I don't, great. I just can't do this anymore; I am sorry. Amen." As soon as I finished, I started to open the bottle of pills when suddenly the phone rang, completely startling me. I was shocked. Who would be calling me? When I answered, it was a familiar voice, a friend I had made in one of the towns I lived in before. She said, "Hi, Joy. How are you doing? I just thought I would check in on how things are going for you in West Palm Beach?"

"I am not doing well right now," I managed to say, choking through my tears. I explained to her about the surgery and how I had just made it home. As it turned out, she was in Las Vegas at the time and had thought of me for some reason and had decided to give me a call. She called her husband right away. He came to my apartment within a couple of hours. He picked me up, took me to their house an hour away, and set up the guest bedroom for me. He helped me get through the worst part of recovering from the surgery, but what he didn't know was that by helping me he had actually saved my life.

The day came for the follow-up appointment with a different doctor. I had no idea what to expect from this appointment; all I knew was that I desperately hoped he had some answers for me. That appointment changed me. It cut me so deeply that I left that place thinking that all my feelings of worthlessness had been confirmed into reality and finalized forever. He told me more about the disease, the horrible details of it, the life of pain that accompanies it for many women, and the reality that I would never be able to have children because of it. He said if I ever wanted to conceive a child that I needed to do certain drug treatments to stop my periods and prevent the spread of the disease for a year. Then, I would have to try to conceive after that year or I never would because the lesions would come back. I was nineteen years old. I didn't even have a boyfriend, and I was supposed to try to conceive in a year or I never could? After all that I had been through, all that I had done, all that had happened to me, and now this. Who would ever want me? If I ever found the right person, once he found out that I was "diseased" and could not have children, it would be all over.

I decided that the drug treatment was the only thing I could do, so I went for it. Big mistake. I got a shot that was supposed to last for a whole month. It did; it was the longest month of my life! I had an allergic reaction to the medication followed by days that I was so sick that I couldn't even get out of bed. There was extreme nausea, weakness, body aches, severe hot flashes, dizziness, and many other strange symptoms. I ended up losing twenty pounds that I really couldn't afford to lose to begin with. No food sounded good to me, and I couldn't go get it if it had.

Once again, I was alone in my apartment trying to survive. More than anything, I felt so badly for my little pup, Killer B. He had so much energy, and I couldn't even take him for walks. He would stay by my side on the air mattress until he couldn't stand it anymore; then he would run around the house like a wild animal as fast as he could. Around and around the entire apartment he would run, lap after lap until he had worn himself out; then back to my side he would go. The spare room became his potty spot, and there was nothing I could do to stop it because I couldn't get up.

There were times when it was too much to take, the sickness, the loneliness; it got to me, and I would just lie there and cry. My sweet, little puppy knew when I had reached that point and would quietly lick my tears. His sweet, little face and the unconditional love he showed melted my heart every time. I was so happy to have him no matter where he went potty; he was a small light in the darkness in which I had found myself. I felt like I had been swallowed up by a heavy sadness that I could not run from, that I could not escape. The word "disease" haunted my thoughts and carried with it a sense of shame, a feeling of isolation and separation from all I had known before and all that I had easily taken for granted. The pain was constant; it would not leave and would not allow me to forget. I knew that I would never be the same; my future seemed so uncertain, yet again. I was desperate for relief, desperate to find some way of escaping the new reality that I faced. So I did what I had done for years, what I had done best—I pretended everything was fine and tried to escape reality.

Chapter 7
Blinding Doubt

"For the message of the cross is foolishness to those who are perishing,
but to us who are being saved it is the power of God."
1 Corinthians 1:18 (NKJV)

March 1999, Grass Valley, California

HOW DID I GET HERE? I am in a church! This is crazy! I hate Christians; they are fake, hypocrites. I don't even believe in their God. If there is a God, where has He been all my life? How could He have let all those things happen to me? No, He can't be real. I shouldn't be here. Why am I here? I felt so awkward in the back of the church. People were looking at me; I knew it. *Why did I let my Mom talk me into going?* Mom was convinced that somehow this would help me, that maybe I could be healed from this incurable affliction I had. *What a dreamer!* I had given up on dreams a long time ago. I remember hearing about this God of love when I was a kid. Every Sunday I heard of Him, but everyday was painfully hard. We were poor; my stepdad was cruel and abusive. He never joined us in going to church every Sunday. The kids at church were also cruel. We didn't have much money, so I never had nice clothes to wear. We would get hand-me-downs from some of the families there. I will never forget wearing some of those clothes to church. I was excited to have them to wear until one of the girls pointed at me and said, "That used to be mine!"

I never wore those hand-me-downs to church again. Instead, I opted for the old uglies. I hated being there, never fitting in, never being accepted. I helped out with the little kids' church more and more, not because I was doing something good but just to get away from my own class and the kids my age. As I heard the stories of this God of love I concluded that He was nothing more than a fairy tale, or if He were real, He did not care about me. There was one teacher who did reach out to me. When she heard that my dad had died, she took me out to dinner at a nice restaurant. I was so excited to be eating at a real restaurant! That was not something we got to do as kids; we could never afford that! I felt bad that I was so happy to get to go, especially since she was doing it because she felt badly that my dad had died. Regardless of the reason, I really enjoyed it. Apart from that, my memories of church were also a source of pain and anger, something I held on to for years, somewhere I told myself I would never go again. Yet, there I was...in a church!

There was some music; then the Pastor shared some things. I don't even remember what; I wasn't really listening. *What could he possibly say that would matter to me? I am not one of "them".* When he was finished, he offered prayer for anyone who needed to be healed. Well, I knew I needed to be healed, so I had nothing to lose. I went up there even though I didn't want to. My mom shared a little about what was wrong with me. The pastor looked at me and said, "I will pray for you, but you do not need physical healing. You need to be healed spiritually." *What? That is crazy! This guy does not have a clue! He doesn't know how much pain I am in! Of course I need to be healed physically. What an idiot! He has no idea!* His words only confirmed to me that church was not where I would find the answers. There had to be another way. I left there convinced I had only wasted my time.

The pain continued wearing down my resolve, my will to fight, and my will to live. After that visit to California, I flew back to Florida more empty than I had begun. Seeing my family, my little brothers, and sisters only tore me up more inside. I missed them. I had missed so much of them, of their childhood. I had not been there for them. I was ashamed that I had not been a good role model, not a good sister. What did I have to show for all my years away? Even the schooling I had worked so hard at was now nothing, gone. I went back to that empty apartment brokenhearted, alone, and aching for more to life, yet knowing deep down that there was no hope for me. The empty apartment was symbolic of what my life had become, a reminder that I had nothing, that I was nothing, and that no matter how hard I tried I would always come up empty. The physical pain tormented me; it mirrored the pain I felt inside, reminding me that I would never be the same, that I was incomplete, that I was wounded, damaged goods, that my dream of being happy would never come true, and that my desire to be loved would never be fulfilled. I was truly alone, and I was drowning in my despair. Yet, somehow I decided that I had to keep going, that I had to keep fighting. I refused to give up and determined that I could not let it end like that. Self pity was my enemy and would swallow me fast. I had made it that far. Quitting was no option, so I was determined to keep going. What other option did I have anyway?

Chapter 8
The Living Dead

"Her feet go down to death, her steps lay hold of hell. Lest you ponder her path of life-her ways are unstable; you do not know them."
Proverbs 5:5-6 (NKJV)

May 1999, West Palm Beach, Florida

HOW DID I GET HERE? I can see the paramedics lifting my body on a stretcher, then starting to carry me out of the nightclub. People were staring and watching them as they moved through the club trying to get my body to the ambulance. I am watching, too! How can I be watching? I don't understand what is happening. Colors are melting, walls bending; everything looks like a cartoon! I can't tell what is real. I can't move. Am I dead? Did I really die? My body is tingling, but it won't move. The sounds of the music are in slow motion except for the constant beat, over and over, so loud I can feel it. I must have overdosed; I must be dead. It is no wonder I overdosed, after taking ecstasy, GHB (Gamma hydroxybutyrate), and special K (a cat tranquilizer) all in the same night. This is it, I finally pushed it to the limit, and it has killed me...something I longed for, yet feared.

My friend walked by and handed me a bottle of water. Although slowly, my hand did move. *I can't be dead! I must have imagined the paramedics and me on the stretcher.* Slowly I took a drink of water. I needed it desperately. My body seemed like it was shutting down. Every movement took such great effort; I felt like I weighed more than my body could move. I could not tell if I was standing or sitting; I could barely function. I could not tell how long I had been there like that. Over time things changed, and I could move, but it still seemed like slow motion. I needed to go to the bathroom but could not imagine how I would ever get there. The distance across the nightclub might as well have been the distance across the Grand Canyon. I couldn't make it there. As the night wore on, I finally had the ability to walk again, although it wasn't easy. Somehow, I survived that night, but the memory of watching my body being carried out on a stretcher stayed with me. Even though it was my imagination or some type of hallucination, it was real and vivid in my mind. Deep down, maybe even subconsciously, I knew it was almost a reality.

I almost overdosed in that nightclub. How tragic it could have been! How it could have ended so quickly. I thought I could run from what I was feeling. Somehow I thought the drugs would ease what I was feeling inside. I thought if I just had enough fun maybe the emptiness would stop. The best the drugs could do was temporarily distract me, but the pain and emptiness always came flooding back, hitting me hard and reminding me that I could never run far enough. I could never escape it; it was a part of me. My life had become an endless search. I was searching, always searching for the next fun thing, the next thing that would get my mind off my reality, and the next thing that would fill the emptiness, but nothing did. Running from reality was all I could do; yet even in running, there was no escape. The physical pain continued to torment me day after day. No drugs eased it; nothing could distract me from it. This "thorn in my side" kept me from enjoying anything.

One day a small light appeared in the dark, a small piece of hope in the form of a packet in the mail. I had forgotten about contacting this particular doctor's office many weeks before. My aunt had told me about a surgeon she had heard of that specialized in the disease I had. He was one of a few doctors who specialized in endometriosis. She also had this same disease but had had a hysterectomy years before to deal with it because there was no cure. The packet gave more information about the disease and why this doctor was having success in how he was treating it. The statistics of the reduction of pain after this surgery were amazing, better than anything I had read, or heard about. It was close to a cure, and some women could even have kids after. I knew he was my hope. This doctor would save me from the nightmare I was living. If he could just take away the pain, I knew I would be okay, that I could make it somehow and that I wouldn't need the drugs anymore. I would be able to function without them and start doing something with my life. I was still young; maybe I could even go back to school and finish what I had started. However, there was a huge obstacle before me...money. I needed money, a lot of money to travel to Oregon and have the surgery. I did not know how I would do it; I just knew that I had to. It was my only hope; this doctor was the only one who could save me.

Chapter 9

Prisoner Set Free

"Therefore if the Son makes you free,
you shall be free indeed."
John 8:36 (NKJV)

July 1999, Grass Valley, California

HOW DID I GET HERE? I am standing in the auditorium of my old junior high school, only now it was being used as a church. I had many bad and good memories there at Lyman Gilmore School. Those were the years I first headed downhill, the first years of getting into harder and harder drugs. My attempts at other things had failed, like trying to fit in, playing sports, getting good grades, working hard, and trying out for cheerleading only to be told that they knew my family couldn't pay for the costs of cheerleading so I wasn't a good fit for the team. I was trying so hard to fit in with the cool kids but never was able to keep up with the new styles of nice clothes that came along with being one of the popular kids. The stoner group had few requirements, the only requirement was being stoned, and that was something that I decided I could fit right in with. Rebellion had settled into my heart, and, like the music I listened to, I was against all authority and was only content when drugs made me comfortably numb, no matter how short lived.

It seemed strange to me that this was my old school, and yet here I stood in this old auditorium for a church service of all things! It looked so different than I remembered; it seemed smaller, much more rundown. I wasn't expecting much to happen that day; my main hope was to get my mom off my back so she would quit asking me to go. I felt a sense of obligation since she had been letting me stay at her house ever since I had moved back from Florida. My hope had been that I would come back to California, find a job, and save enough money to get the surgery in Oregon that I desperately needed. After that, my plan was to move to Hawaii where my older sister lived, and, if the big Y2K end of the world disaster happened that everyone was talking about, I wouldn't care because I would die in paradise. A good plan I thought, but things never seemed to go as I planned in life.

Instead, I made it to California on a flight with my little Pomeranian; my car was being shipped and would be there in two weeks. Somehow my car was lost and didn't arrive when it was supposed to, and I couldn't find a job anywhere! I did not have enough money to pay for my car when it finally arrived, so I was completely stressed out. The pain in my abdomen continually got worse and so intense that I could barely stand up straight. Having no idea what I would do, I was completely discouraged. Then there was my mom who would pray for me and beg me to come to church, as if that could possibly help all the problems I faced!

One Wednesday night when I had nothing to do and I wasn't high, I decided to go with her to this church. It was awkward, but I managed through it and even paid attention this time. It was so strange; it was all about end of time prophecy. I had heard about those end of the world things that people talked about, but this was the first time that I had heard about it from the Bible. I had never really believed the Bible was true. I had not read it or anything (apart from Sunday school as a child), but I had heard many strange opinions on it. Some said it was something made up by the government in a conspiracy to keep people distracted. Another was that it was written by aliens to brainwash people...who knows! I had heard many things about it, but I had decided it was nothing more than fairy tales like the ones I had read when I was little, the ones that never come true. Yet for the first time, I was hearing it talk about the things happening in my lifetime, in the current world around me; yet it had been written so long ago. I wasn't sure what I thought after that night; I just had a very uncomfortable feeling. *What if the Bible was true?*

Pretending like what I had heard didn't matter, I kept smoking pot acting like I was all right. I acted normal when I would see my old friends, but the sharp, stabbing pain in my side wouldn't let me forget no matter how much pot I smoked. Things kept getting worse; I knew I was going to go crazy long before I could ever make it to Oregon. I couldn't keep going on like that. *Even if I found a job, how could I work in this condition?* My mom kept insisting that I go with her on a Sunday morning where they met at my old school. I wasn't sure what difference that would make, but I went anyway, despite the many doubts I had.

As I stood there, the music started playing. It was strangely familiar, but I wasn't sure why. All I knew was it brought tears to my eyes. I felt so heavy, so sad, and so broken. I was such an incomplete person, a shell that outwardly looked all right but shattered inwardly. I had trouble controlling my tears; each song that played brought a different level of sorrow to my heart. When the pastor came up, I sat and listened. It was different this time; it was as if he was just speaking to me. He spoke of many things like sin and how it would destroy us by its very nature. He spoke of forgiveness, and how God's grace to us was the sacrifice of Jesus. I do not remember everything that was said that day, but I do remember that it felt like God was speaking directly to me. He was reaching out His hand to me, offering to forgive me. He knew all that I had done and all that had been done to me, but He still loved me and wanted to give me a new life. After the pastor taught, he had everyone stand up, and the worship team came up and played more music.

The pastor said they were going to take communion in remembrance of what Christ had done to pay for our sins. The pastor said that it was important to not take communion in an unworthy manner. He said that if you were not a believer of Jesus or if you had unconfessed sin in your heart then it would not be for you; it was for believers only. However, he said that if you were willing to confess your sins and turn to Jesus then you were welcome to join them in partaking of the communion. I didn't know what that meant, but I knew I had sin in my heart. As communion was being passed out, I decided at that moment to ask God to forgive me. As the music played, I prayed quietly in my mind, *"Please, God, forgive me. I know that I have made a mess of my life. I am sorry. If You are real, and if this is true, please forgive me. You can have my life... the mess that it is... if You want it, but please take it all because I can't handle it anymore!"* I took the little cracker and the tiny cup of juice when everyone else did. After the service, I talked with a few people who recognized me from when I was a kid. They were very friendly and welcoming. I didn't notice it at first, but I had this strange feeling inside. I had a feeling of unexplainable peace, a peace that everything was going to be alright. Although my problems were not gone, I did not feel stressed, just peace.

Later that day, I noticed how different everything seemed. I felt so light, I felt like a giant burden of weight had been lifted off my shoulders. I just kept smiling all day; I felt so happy. I didn't understand why, but somehow I knew that God really did love me, that He had not forgotten me, and that if I died right then it would be okay because I was forgiven. That afternoon I sat on my mom's porch while smoking a cigarette and thought about what had happened that day and how differently everything looked to me. It was then that I noticed...my pain...it was gone! I held my breath for a second, expecting it to come back, but it did not; it was gone! *How was this possible?* For the next few days, I kept waiting for it to come back, thinking at any moment the pain would return as it had always done, but that time it did not come back. I had been healed! My painful, incurable disease was gone.

Chapter 10
Sharing Freedom

"For I am not ashamed of the gospel of Christ,
for it is the power of God to salvation for everyone who believes..."
Romans 1:16 (NKJV)

August 1999, Grass Valley, California

HOW DID I GET HERE? I am standing in front of the Wayne Brown Correctional Facility, trembling and waiting to be let in so I could see my brother Matt and tell him I was a Christian now. Me, a Christian! The thought seemed almost comical as I spent so many years despising Christians, judging them, and deeming them ignorant and foolish to believe such lies written in a book of fairy tales. Yet, here I was proudly taking the title "Christian", having been forever changed by calling out to Christ. After being set free from all the pain and bondage that held me down, not to mention the painful and incurable disease I had, I was not the same person anymore. My life wasn't even mine anymore; I knew that much, and I was glad that it was now under the control of the God who loved me and not my own self-destructive hands. I stood there trembling, knowing that I had to go in there. Despite not knowing how he'd respond, I had to tell my brother that Jesus was real and that He had given me a new life. I was so nervous to see my brother again! What would he say when I told him? Would he think I was crazy? It sounded crazy, but it was real, more real than anything I had ever experienced. I had to tell him what happened to me no matter what he thought, but the nerves were getting to me! Although it had been so long since I had seen him, our relationship was such that no matter how long we had been apart we were always as close as ever once we talked. Surely he would be happy for me if nothing else, but I was afraid to tell him. So far, few people shared my excitement when I told them; some even ridiculed me and argued with me how foolish it all was, only adding to the fear that my brother would do the same. Finally the doors opened, and I was let into a series of holding rooms before I finally got to the room where we would have our visit. I sat at a table and waited with other people who were also waiting.

Walking toward me, his eyes lit up when he saw me; he looked healthy, much better than he did the last time I had seen him in Florida. I was so happy to see him. He started asking me about some guys in there he thought that I knew, but I didn't really care about people I used to know because I was overly anxious to tell him who I knew now. As soon as there was an opening, I did it; I told him what had happened to me! I probably spoke so fast because I was scared that he would stop me to tell me how dumb I was. I told him how I came to Christ, how He healed my incurable disease, how my pain was gone, how I had been set free from drugs, and how I had a peace never known before. He sat there looking at me, stunned. When I stopped talking, I just waited for his reaction, not sure how he would respond. Regardless, I was very relieved that it was finally out.

The response I got was not one I expected. He told me that about nine months before that day he had started going to church. There was a young guy he had met who would pick him up and take him to church services. He said that he had given his life to Christ and even gotten baptized. I was shocked! I couldn't believe it; he was a Christian, too! He said that he had done well for a while but then had made the stupid choice to start smoking pot again. He stopped going to church and eventually ended up getting into trouble and landing back in jail. He looked me straight in the eyes and said, "I know God is real now, Joy; I can see the change in you. You are different; you are not the same person." I left that place so happy; I knew that God could do for my brother what He had done for me, and that meant so much to me. Matt meant so much to me.

Matt always came in and out of my life throughout the years as he was trying to find his own way. Our bond never broke; we always loved each other and would always try to help and parent one another whenever we were near each other or whenever we talked. He battled with addictions, with anger, and with choices that usually ended up putting him in jail. He would have seasons of sobriety and would accomplish great things but would always, somehow, get pulled back.

He had even come out to Florida in hope of a better life. He, too, had tried living with my step dad but ended up on the streets after one drunken night our step dad pulled a gun on my brother. Matt called and asked me to come get him. Matt had been convinced that our stepdad was crazy enough to pull that trigger, and he couldn't go back there. I went and got him immediately and brought him home to stay with me at my place. Once my boyfriend got home from work, I soon discovered that he had no place in his heart for my family. He wanted complete control of me and demanded that I get rid of Matt or he would kill him. My brother could fight, and I knew it could get ugly. However, at the time he had a hurt wrist, and I feared who would win; there was no good outcome. So in genuine fear for my brother's life, I took him to town and dropped him off, not knowing where he would go. I will never forget that feeling, that torment, my heart being ripped out. My brother meant more to me than my boyfriend, but I was trapped. At the time, I thought I had no choice. Ironically, what my boyfriend made me do by getting rid of the only real family member I had in that state actually had the opposite effect of his intentions. He was trying to keep me under his control, but, instead, a seed of bitterness was planted that day in my heart. That seed grew into a tree of hatred toward him that would eventually mature enough that I would finally leave him.

Matt had managed to get by and had landed on his feet. Ironically, the street I dropped him off was near where the same young couple that had helped me out years before had moved. Matt met Nick somewhere previously and had become friends. When I dropped him off, he started walking then he happened to see Nick outside of his house. They talked and Nick let him stay with them for a little while until he found a job and another place to live. Sadly, the pull of addictions eventually got the best of him, followed by another series of bad choices that sent him to jail. At that time in 1998, jail for him meant getting shipped back to California. After serving some time, he went to rehab where he met the young man who started picking him up for church. It was this young man who really reached out to Matt and spent many hours talking with him, encouraging him to come to Christ, and praying with him.

After the day I saw him at the jail, a new season started in his life, as well as mine. It was like trees at the end of winter that look cold and dead but suddenly start to show new life. The new life I saw in him was amazing to see. When he got out of jail, I invited him to move in with me. The Lord had already blessed me with a job and then a little apartment to rent behind my mom's house in California. We spent the next nine or ten months learning and growing in our faith. We would stay up late talking about life, reading the Bible, and watching videos that gave scientific or historical evidence to our faith. He would write worship songs, and we would stay up singing them or having friends over who enjoyed those same things. We would pray together, seeking God's help in our needs and for the people He would put in our path. We would get to see God answer, God provide, and God move in many situations. We frequently went street witnessing, and I really enjoyed hearing my brother share the Gospel with people he would meet or old friends with whom he used to party. Matt had a way about him; he was very smart and memorized Scripture so easily. He always seemed to know what to say and was so convincing that I saw even the hardest of hearts soften when he spoke. I witnessed souls enter the kingdom through my brother; I saw such compassion in him that he never had before. He cared more for others' sufferings because he had suffered so much in life. The light in his eyes shone brighter in those days than it ever had before or ever would again. It was just like the blossoms on the fruit trees in spring and how they give such a sweet fragrance for a short time. That short season was the sweetest in our lives, and I cherish remembering it. Sadly, spring doesn't last; no season does, and I remember clearly when the harsh heat of summer came.

I had gotten a weekend job selling self tanner for a beauty company out of Los Angeles and started traveling a lot. I would get home from an out of town trade show and find out Matt would get high while I was gone. He could never lie to me and would always tell me right away if he had blown it. He became so miserable; the light in his eyes started to fade, and all sense of joy and peace was gone. I did not know it at the time but by using the drugs he had opened himself up to demonic attack. The Bible speaks of drugs as witchcraft, and it opens you up to a demonic influence. Looking back now, I can see that influence so clearly. It got to the point that I was scared to leave him home alone, but I had to work; that job was paying our rent. I came home after one of those trips, and we got into a fight. He was justifying his actions, and I was angry at him. I couldn't understand how after being set free from that stuff that he could go back! The fight got ugly, and he threw things around, breaking them. Remembering the life I had lived with a violent man, I snapped and screamed at him. He rushed toward me, grabbing me by the neck and pinning me against the wall. I will never forget the rage in his eyes. I could not see any of the blue, only his black pupils. They were so full of darkness that it was like being face to face with a demon. A familiar flashback of my ex-boyfriend's violent darkness came over me. He did and said some of the exact things; then he let go, dropped me to the ground, and left. I wept that night; it felt as though my brother had died and I was mourning his death. Soon after that night, he called me and apologized for how he had acted, but it wasn't the same after that. He could barely look me in the eyes. He ended up moving out, saying he was going to live with his girlfriend.

Our relationship was still close, and I loved him as much as ever, but something did die that night. It was like a slow moving cancer had made its way into his heart, and it wouldn't stop growing until it had completely consumed him. One day it would.

Chapter 11
New Creation

"Therefore, if anyone is in Christ, he is a new creation;
old things have passed away;
behold, all things have become new."
2 Corinthians 5:17 (NKJV)

September 1999, Grass Valley, California

HOW DID I GET HERE? I am standing face-to-face with the man who assaulted and raped me when I was fifteen years old. For many years, my hatred of this man ran deep. I wanted him dead, I would have killed him myself if I could have. What he did sent me on a tailspin of drug use that nearly killed me as I wanted to end my life everyday. Attempting to numb the pain, trying to just forget, but how could I ever forget? I was not expecting to ever see him again, yet here I was face-to-face with him after five years.

By a miracle and through my new best friend Tammy, I had landed a new job with the county. She was another young woman who had recently come to Christ and had her life transformed. We were both so excited about our faith, so excited to share with everyone we came in contact with because we had both been prisoners but were now set free. God was moving in my life daily; old things were passing away, and I was becoming a new person! He had healed my physical body of an incurable disease. He had healed my broken heart, forgiven me, and taken the heavy burden of sin off me. Even my desire to use drugs was gone! Daily, I would pray to God with the problems I faced, and daily He answered. I had my car, an apartment, and now a good job. I was excited about the future for the first time in my life.

At my job, I was involved in an outreach program to the community for low income medical insurance. As a part of the job, we could hire trustees from the jail to do physical labor. Trustees were inmates who were on good behavior and trusted to go work at various places with county staff then be returned to the jail. Tammy and I had been anticipating this day for weeks. We knew that we would have two trustees helping us, so we prayed and prayed that we could share Jesus and His power to forgive and set people free with these guys. We decided that she would have one guy in her car and I would have the other. The day finally came when we both picked them up and headed to our sight. The entire way I talked with this guy about Jesus. He had said that he was a believer but that he had fallen back into drugs and gotten into trouble. He had a wife and two children and felt so horrible about his mistakes. We had a great conversation about God's forgiveness the whole way there.

Once we got there, we got right to work; a little later I decided I would go buy everyone a soda, so I went to ask him his name then see what he wanted to drink. When he said his name, the strangest thing happened. It was as if blinders came off my eyes, and I suddenly recognized him! It was him! Standing in front of me was the man who had hurt me all those years ago. I turned around quickly and walked away, not sure what I should do. My heart was pounding, and I was shaking. I felt like I wanted to throw up. *Do I freak out and attack this guy? Do I yell at him for what he did and all the pain it caused? What should I do?* Once the shock started to wear off, I tried to find anger. I tried to find the hatred I had for him, but couldn't; I only felt compassion. I felt sorry for him. I prayed and asked God what I should be feeling? I should have been angry, but I wasn't! I searched my heart and found only love where anger had once ruled. A Scripture verse came to my mind at that moment: "Therefore, if anyone is in Christ, he is a new creation; old things have passed away, behold, all things have become new."—2 Corinthians 5:17

In that moment, I knew I had become a new creation in Christ. I was not the same person that he had hurt so long ago; I was a new person! At that moment I also had a choice. I could have dug up the pain of the person I used to be, or I could let it go because the person I had become need not feel that hurt anymore. The old Joy didn't live anymore, and she died the day I gave my life to Jesus. All that pain, sorrow, shame, and regret died with her. I had been born again. I prayed and asked God to help me and to give me the strength to walk as a new person. I also asked Him to not allow the man to recognize me. I went back as though nothing had happened, but I knew so much had.

We finished the set up, then headed back to the jail without him recognizing me. I am not sure if he didn't know who I was because of how different I looked or if God had prevented him, but I was thankful. I will never forget our return trip. He talked a lot more than I did this time; he shared many things. He spoke of a young man that was in jail with him. He said this young man was messed up on drugs, and he blamed himself for it. He had been the one to give this guy drugs for the first time a few years back, so he said that he felt like it was his fault that he was this way, that he was responsible because he had introduced him.

At that moment, I realized that this man carried such regret for the things he had done. I knew then that if he carried regret for giving a guy drugs then he carried regret for what he had done to me. I felt a sense of closure with that, a final seal to the coffin of my old life. I was miraculously and truly free from the pain and was able to let that all go—something I would have missed if I had lost it on him instead of trusting the Lord. When we pulled up to the jail, he turned and looked at me with tears in his eyes and said, "You have been such an answer to my prayers; thank you." I prayed for him; he got out of my car, and I never saw him again.

Chapter 12
Voices of Darkness

"For we do not wrestle against flesh and blood,
but against principalities, against powers, against the rulers of
the darkness of this age, against spiritual hosts of wickedness
in the heavenly places."
Ephesians 6:12 (NKJV)

April 2001, Canao, Philippines

HOW DID I GET HERE? I am surrounded by darkness and smoke, completely terrified as the distorted faces of the villagers looked at me through the shadows, waiting for me to speak. It was so dark that I couldn't see everyone in the room! I had been asked by our missions team leader to share my testimony to a group of youth in a small village in the mountains of the Philippines. I had been told it would be a youth group, but the people who came were ages of three through ninety plus! I could only make out some women and children, but there were people sitting everywhere. With the villagers perfectly blending into the dark, I could even still see them climbing in through the window, the only window. The air was hot and humid, and there was only one, little, kerosene candle to light the room—that was until a woman brought in a burning piece of wood to help with the lighting. Even so, it only filled the room with smoke. I knew I had to get up to speak, but I did not know how I could. This was one of the biggest opportunities I could have ever asked for, but here I was frozen in fear!

The country of the Philippines had never really been on my radar, until a man from my church who had been actively involved with ministering in the Philippines for many years had organized a trip. After much prayer I really believed the Lord wanted me to be a part of it. Although mostly a medical mission, (I wasn't a doctor or a nurse) my focus was more on helping with the clinics and evangelism. It was a 6 week trip starting in Manila and working our way around the main island of the Philippines. Along the way we would stay in several different Youth With A Mission Bases and hire some of them to be interpreters for us as we did ministry. Our intention here was to provide medical clinics, treating the sick who lived in this small, isolated village who did not have access to medical care. There was a group of seven Americans (myself included) , three translators and our driver who had brought medical supplies and toiletries to this village in the mountains.

Our team had traveled for days to get to this isolated village in the ancient rice terraces of the Philippines. It had been years since any white people had been there, and we were the first, white missionaries to go there thanks to a newly completed road (or what they considered a road). The road did not even go all the way into the village, we still had to hike for a while on the rice terraces to get there. It was one of the most beautiful places I had ever seen. The village rested on the side of a mountain, and the houses were all stacked so close to each other. A beautiful river flowed into the canyon, and the bright green rice terraces were cut perfectly into the sides of all the hills. They were everywhere, even up to the mountaintops. Things were lush and green, full of beauty, and rich with wonder of how on earth they ever built the terraces on the mountains like that! The air was so much cleaner and fresher than in Manila where the toxic fumes and the smell of diesel and waste were as heavy as the humidity that filled the air. I was so excited to be there, looking forward to what God had in store for us.

It was almost dark when we arrived at the village on Good Friday 2001, so we set up our air mattresses in the host house. Thankfully, this house was beside the only toilet in the village which was owned by the Barungi Captain, leader of the village. This "toilet" was nothing more than a small, shack-like room attached to the side of his house. It was so small that I had to squeeze to get in it and contained nothing more than a hole in the ground to squat over. However, this was something to be thankful for indeed! Our team leader then asked me if I would be willing to share my testimony that night at a youth group. They had a village community meeting room where I could speak. It was something for which I had prayed and longed. I desperately wanted to share the amazing things God had done in my life. I went for a walk alone to spend time in prayer and to prepare myself, but nothing could have prepared me for the evil I was about to face.

I knew that God had called me on this trip to the Philippines. He had proven it to me over and over, so I had no doubt. It was that knowledge that helped me push through the hardest things. I remembered the day the money was due for the trip's airfare. The deadline had been 2:00 p.m., and I was $275 short. I had looked at the clock around 11:00 a.m. and knew I did not have it and did not know how I could get it in time! I sat in my little cubicle at work and said one final prayer. "Okay God, You know the deadline is very soon. Please, if You want me to go, somehow provide the money. If not, I know it is not Your will for me, no matter how badly I want to do it." A little bit later the phone rang. It was a guy from AutoZone. He apologized for the delay, and wanted me to know that my check was ready. *My check? What check?* Then I remembered.

About five months before, our little town had a freak snowstorm. I had gone into AutoZone to get snow cables for my car. Of course, I did not know the first thing about putting snow cables on a car, so the attendant was nice enough to put them on for me. Unfortunately, he did not know how to put them on either and did it incorrectly, causing them to snap while I was driving. Without warning as I was driving during the storm, I lost control of the steering but miraculously in a spot with a small turn out. I pulled over and called a tow truck. The next day after the roads had been plowed, I got into my car and drove away. What I did not know, but found out rather quickly, was that when the snow cable snapped it had cut my brake line. As I drove through the red light unable to stop, I became very appreciative of the fact that I was in a small town and that few people were even out because of the weather, so I made it through the signal without a collision. Again, I had to call a tow truck but this time had it towed to be repaired. As eventful as all of that was, I really had forgotten all about the whole thing. However, a few hours before my last payment for the airfare to the Philippines was due, my reimbursement for my cut brake line was ready for me to come and get. I didn't know they were actually going to reimburse me. After the whole ordeal, I felt obligated to call them and let them know that attendants should be properly trained before installing them on cars. I did not ask them to compensate me but I was more than happy to come and get this reimbursement that happened to be the exact amount I still needed for my airfare.

So there I was, thousands of miles away from home in an isolated village on the beautiful mountains of the Philippines about to share my testimony to the people of the village...a dream come true, really! I knew I was to do this; I had done it before, yet I had never felt so afraid. The fear was paralyzing; it took all my strength just to stand up, but somehow I had to speak! Once I finally started, each word was a struggle, as though choking on them yet trying to grasp each word in order to speak them. The long pauses as the interpreter would translate what I said into their own language felt like hours! I kept stumbling over my words and losing my train of thought. My eyes were burning from the smoke; I could barely breathe. The voices were the hardest part! The sound of voices in the dark, whispers tormenting me. As the interpreter would speak, I was bombarded with thoughts like: *"Why did you say that?!" You fool, you are failing! You are letting the whole team down!"* Some of the babies were crying, others even peeing on the floor. The stench of sweat, kerosene, and smoke in the hot, dark room made each passing moment feel like endless torture.

Finally, after finishing my testimony, I shared the message of the Gospel. I shared that although we had all sinned against a holy and perfect God, He loved us and provided a way for us to be forgiven. Because it was the Good Friday in 2001, it was close to 2000 years since He had sent His Son to die in our place. I testified that because of His sacrifice our debt for sin had been paid, we can have a relationship with Him in this life, and heaven can become our home. I asked if anyone wanted to receive this forgiveness God was offering them through His Son. In a moment of silence after I gave the invitation to accept Jesus, I stood there completely doubting that after my utter failure to communicate my testimony anyone would want to receive Christ.

Discouragement had so clouded my mind that when seven elderly women came forward, I didn't really believe what they were doing. I even asked them again to be sure. What these women did was far beyond what we even understood. Breaking a chain of paganism and idol worship by stepping forward to accept Jesus Christ as their Savior and Lord was something foreign to those of us from America. On the other side of the planet in a world so different from anything I had ever known, somehow I was there as a small tool in the hands of a great and mighty God who truly does care about His creation. I was again reminded of His power and His ability to draw people to Himself, with or without our participation!

That night I couldn't shake the thoughts and the feelings of completely failing, as if it were somehow about me! I confessed to my team that I was sorry about how badly it went. They assured me that they thought it went great and did not notice the things I was talking about. *Were they in the same room?* It was almost like we had seen two, very different things take place. I felt reassured at first but then was easily able to tell myself they were just being nice. *You failed*! Once I went to bed, the night seemed to last forever. I couldn't sleep; I was continually tormented. I felt so ashamed and so condemned that by morning I had decided I should probably never share my testimony again! After breakfast I broke down, crying and telling the team how I felt and the night I had had. They decided I needed prayer, so they laid hands on me and prayed. I had such a sense of relief after that prayer, and my outlook completely changed! There was a heaviness that left me after that; I knew that what had happened the night before was spiritual warfare. My thinking was clear again, and I knew that what had taken place the night before was not about me or how good or bad I had done but about the breaking of chains for the seven women who came forward. It was about the "whosoever would believe in Him" by the preaching of the Gospel. I was able to recognize the torment and my negative thoughts as clearly coming from the enemy who did not want anyone being set free. His tight grip had been on this village for many years, especially in the hearts of the men who practiced dark rituals and animal sacrifices to their gods and idols. The enemy never releases his territories without a fight.

Even though there were many ups and downs, many challenges, and many new things I had never seen or experienced before, that trip was still an incredible experience for me. Seeing God's hand move in many ways and seeing the spiritual attacks of the enemy in ways new to me opened my eyes. The people impacted me forever; their poverty was so overwhelming, yet the love of them had won my heart. The Filipinos were humble, simple, and happy; they knew no other life, so they had nothing to compare it to. They didn't need the many things for which we Americans strive; family was more important than possessions; the elderly didn't even keep track of their age! Seeing miracles happen and experiencing God using me to love and speak to people unlike anyone I had ever met helped me to bond to them instantly. He showed me that all people are precious to Him and just how small the world is to Him.

One night we were having dinner at the house of the leader of the YWAM (Youth With A Mission) base where we were staying. Through conversation at dinner, I found out that thirty years before this same man was the interpreter for my aunt and uncle when they were in the

Philippines working with the people who lived in the garbage dumps. After translating for them as they shared the Gospel, he had given his life to Christ! All these years later, God had done amazing things in this man's life, and he had gone from living in the garbage dumps to becoming the leader of the YWAM base in Manila. Only God knew that we would discover this connection while having a meal together.

My last week there, my team had already left for the States, and I had stayed behind for another week. I was left with the task of delivering the last of the medications and supplies to the homes of everyone who had been seen and diagnosed. The day after they left I woke up terribly sick and couldn't get out of bed. I was so upset and disappointed. I did not understand why God would allow me to be sick when He knew I had so much work to do!

Later that afternoon, I started to feel better and was able to get out of bed. When I went into the living area of the base, everyone was around the television watching the news. As it turned out, there were upcoming elections, and, due to much corruption in the government, there were people rioting in the streets. Then it hit me; the riots were exactly where I would have been that day had I been feeling well. God spared me unimaginable difficulty by keeping me there that day and not allowing me to be caught in the middle of the chaos and violence. The next day everything had settled down; I felt great and was able to finish the work that needed to be done. I truly learned that God does things in ways we do not understand and that He knows exactly what He is doing.

I knew for sure after that trip that I wanted to be a missionary; I wanted to live a life completely sold out for the Lord. I wanted to be part of bringing people into the kingdom of God, a part of seeing them delivered and set free the way I had been. Sadly, so many of my years had been wasted on myself, living for whatever felt good and for nothing that truly mattered. I was determined that I would never waste my time getting married or having kids (I couldn't have them anyway), but instead I would be a missionary somewhere where the need was great and the workers were few. I had been forever ruined for the ordinary life, and there was no going back.

Chapter 13
Relentless Love

"Trust in the Lord with all of your heart,
and lean not on your own understanding;
in all your ways acknowledge Him,
and He shall direct your paths."
Proverbs 3:5-6 (NKJV)

June 2001, Grass Valley, California

HOW DID I GET HERE? I can't get this guy out of my head! I don't want to get married; I don't want to settle down; I want to be a missionary! I want to be a mother to the orphans in Africa who have lost their parents to AIDS, to love those who have no one, and to share hope to the hopeless. My own thoughts betrayed me daily, betraying my hopes and dreams and pulling me down a road I had no intention of going...marriage! *Everywhere I go I am reminded of this guy.* Daily I was praying that God would just take him out of my thoughts. *I don't want the distraction; I know what I want, and this is not a part of MY plans.*

It all started when my church planned a mission trip to Africa with a few other local churches in the area. I wasn't able to go but I attended the service that was held for them to share about what happened on the trip. I sat and listened to each person speak about the trip and what they got out of it, *then he went up.* I recognized him; we had actually gone to school together when we were kids. He looked much different than I remembered him; he had grown up. There was a light in his eyes that I had never seen before. He had always been sort of a bully in school, and I had always avoided him at all cost. He shared about his experience on the mission trip and talked about playing with the orphan children. My heart was fluttering as he spoke because I did not know that there were Christian men who actually felt like I did about serving God; he even loved the orphans. He was cute and funny; however, what was really noticeable was that he loved the Lord.

As he shared, I thought to myself: *If I ever did get married, I would want to marry a guy like him.* Of course, I knew that would never happen, but it was the first time he made it into my mind, and I had no idea how hard it would be to get him out! Afterwards we chatted a bit, reintroducing ourselves to each other. His name was Aaron Sidebottom. We remembered each other from grade school and now shared a common interest in sharing Christ at a local drug rehab. He said he knew my brother who was at that rehab at the time. That was all; I did not see him again for a very long time, but I thought of him often. In fact, every time that I was successful at not thinking about him anymore, his name would come up. At the grocery store, someone mentioned his name, at the dentist, at church, at a prayer meeting; on and on it went. One day I was having a conversation with my pastor when he interrupted himself just to tell me, "You know who would be perfect for you? This one guy, Aaron Sidebottom." I was so shocked; I don't think I said anything. I prayed for a good month to get him out of my head.

Another time, I was having a conversation with my mom about not giving her any grandkids but that instead of marriage and children I would be a missionary in Africa. She looked at me and said, "Well, if you ever did get married, I would want you to marry this one guy, Aaron Sidebottom."

Clearly I was fighting a battle I could not win; I was surrounded! However, time went on, and a year and a half passed without even seeing him, yet I continually battled to not think about him. Finally, it became a distant thought, and my plans for being a missionary became my focus. I was making arrangements to go to an orphanage in Mozambique, Africa, and had even started trying to learn the Swahili language.

I was at a friend's wedding, when out of nowhere, there he was! My heart skipped a beat; I couldn't believe he was there! I did my best not to look at him; I even avoided being anywhere he was. I kept praying that God would help me not to be distracted; I didn't need this kind of temptation. My mind was made up. *Wasn't it? Yes, it was! That is the end of it!* I left that place so proud of myself for resisting the temptation of talking to him, as if that made me really strong.

A couple weeks later, I was tested again as I was walking through the parking lot of Kmart while he was walking out the store as I was entering. I quickly moved to the other side so as not to let him see me and to avoid any possible conversation. *Wow, so spiritual!* Again I found myself praying against the thoughts that flooded in, the what ifs. I refused to let myself go down that road because I thought it could never really happen for me. For one thing, I had been so hurt before that the idea of it ever happening again was too much, and the harsh reality was no decent guy would ever like me anyway because I had too many scars.

One day I was at the gym, and I went to the drinking fountain to fill up my bottle. I turned to the fountain just as a guy was finishing a drink and standing up; we nearly crashed into each other! We were inches apart, then I realized it was Aaron! Of all the people in the world, it was Aaron Sidebottom. I was scared to death and had no idea what to say, so I acted casually and said, "Don't I know you?" He smiled, and it was all over then. While there, we kept running into each other. We would conveniently end up working out on machines by each other and would have many conversations. I would always look for him when I went there, and suddenly I was able to make it to the gym more often than ever in my entire life! My living situation had changed, and I had moved back into my mom's house temporarily. I would come home from the gym, and my siblings would mock me if I was happy, "You saw Aaron again didn't you?"... Or if I was down, "Aaron wasn't there was he?" There was no hiding it anymore.

My mom had remarried in November of 2001 and left me to watch my four siblings while she was on her honeymoon. After work I went to the gym as I always did and spent extra time on a machine next to him. We were deep in conversation as he walked me out to my car. The parking lot was covered in ice! We both nearly slipped. He offered to follow me home to make sure I made it safely. As I was driving, I called my siblings and panically said, "Hurry up and clean the house! Aaron is coming over!" When we made it there, I asked him if he wanted to come in and meet my siblings. He said he actually remembered them from a few years back when my mom had gone to his church for a while. We made it into the house, and, of course, it was a complete disaster! I looked at the faces of my little brothers and sisters, scolding them with my eyes. I knew by their stunned reaction at seeing Aaron come in that they didn't believe me when I had called. They thought I was lying just to get them to clean up...not a bad idea if it would have worked...and they stood there shocked in disbelief. As the weeks went on and as we spent more time together, a heavy cloud hung over me. I knew that if he found out the things I had been through and the things I had done he would not want anything to do with me. It tormented me daily. I was afraid of it ending because, surprisingly, I had started to dream it could happen for me; I could finally find love.

The day came when I knew I had to tell him. We went for a long walk, and I choked every time I almost said it. Finally as we were close to my house, I decided it was better to end it than to go on any further. I told him about my past; I told him of the things that had happened to me and the things that I had done. I waited for his response knowing that it would be too much for him...Lord knows it was too much for me all those years. He paused, then thoughtfully said, "I believe what the Bible says; you are a new creation in Christ." I couldn't believe it! It was too good to be true, so out came the next one—that would get him for sure! I told him about my physical problems and that I had been told since I was nineteen years old that I could never have children, so if he wanted kids I was not the one for him. He paused, then replied, "If it is God's will, we will have kids; if not, we can adopt." I was shocked! I could not believe that he was not scared off. He had his chance to run away if he couldn't handle it, and he didn't.

It was not very long until we were engaged. Our wedding was set for October 5th, 2002. We knew it was right; everyone around us seemed to know, too. After my experience of trying to pray him away, I knew that God had, in fact, been trying to tell me something but I had been too stubborn to hear it. I had my mind made up without even considering God had other plans for me. My fears had limited what I thought God could do in my life, but God is not limited by my fears or doubts. He is limited by no one. Through my stubbornness and God's persistence, it did help to confirm in me what His will was, and this was clearly it. I learned so much about the tenderness of the Heavenly Father in that time. As we planned for a wedding we could not afford, God showed me how much He cared for me. He even cared about the details. There were things that I wanted but never said out loud, yet God provided them. There were things that we needed, and God provided them in humorous ways over and over again.

One time I was looking for a certain color of candles to go with the other ones we had, and I walked into a store only to find the exact color, the exact amount I needed, and, of course, they were on clearance. My sisters and I went to a store downtown that was going out of business and noticed there were four wedding dresses in the back. I tried on two and found the perfect one, and, of course, it was half off. Aaron's grandma Meme asked him if he wanted his grandpa's wedding ring, and I could have hers. It was such a special gift to Aaron; he had loved his papa so much. When he told me, I was so touched that she would do that, but I admit I was also a little scared. You see, I had pictured a small, simple, dainty ring as my wedding ring. I did not want anything flashy or big, but small and delicate. Aaron's mom loved big jewelry, so I was frightened that his grandma did, too, and I would be a terrible person if I turned it down! We went to her house to look at the rings. I was completely nervous but didn't dare say anything! When I held the ring, I wanted to cry; it was exactly what I had wanted, just what I had pictured—small, simple, yet beautiful. It even fit me! Again, God reminded me that He loved me; that He cared about the things that I cared about; and that He would provide my needs, and even sometimes my wants, because He loved me.

His love never failed and it was relentless. He knew that I was afraid to step out and trust a man after all I had been through, but He wasn't really asking me to trust a man. He was asking me to trust Him. He wanted me to trust Him completely with my life, with my future, my dreams, my hopes, my fears, my everything. He would not be put into a box of my limitations. He was far greater than I could ever know, and He was not limited to what I considered impossible. There was a hard road that lay ahead of me, and He was the only one who could see it. He knew what I needed to make it through it all and gave me confirmations of His will ahead of time so when the seas would get rough (and, boy, they did) I had a sure and strong anchor in the storm.

Chapter 14
The Joys of Sorrow

"And we know that all things work
together for good for those who love God,
to those who are the called according to His purpose."
Romans 8:28 (NKJV)

May 2005, Bend, Oregon

HOW DID I GET HERE? I am alone, lying on a table in the middle of the operating room. It's so cold in here, so bright, so sterile. The people in scrubs came in, put music on, and organized their instruments. They casually chatted with each other, then one by one surrounded me. My heart was racing as they stood there looking at me, waiting for the anesthesia to work so they could cut me open and remove what they believed to be causing my pain, an ovary. As I believed this to be the last chance to remove "the problem", I had been desperate to put an end to whatever was wrong with me. My dream of living a "normal" life, one free from pain, was all I could hope for.

Aaron and I had only been married for a year and a half when I started having health problems. It started out small but grew continually until it was an all consuming storm in my life. Days were filled with headaches, dizziness, and nausea, mimicking pregnancy symptoms but not pregnant. The pain was the hardest to handle. At first it was easy to ignore it; it was something that would come for a few days then go away.

One time the pain didn't go away for a few weeks, so I went to a doctor to see what was happening. After an ultrasound, she saw a cyst, my first of many. She monitored it, and eventually it did go away. One thing I will never forget was what that doctor said after looking at my health history. She said, "Oh, you have endometriosis. That must be it; you know there is no cure for that right?" That same statement would be repeated by many doctors...in fact, every doctor that looked at my history. In my heart I wanted to scream out: NO! God healed me! Then the thought would come into my mind: *Did He? What if He didn't? Why the pain now? What if He just took the pain for a while until my faith in Him was stronger?*

The questions plagued me constantly despite desperately wanting to believe He had healed me, but soon doubt would settle in again. After nearly five years of not having pain, I truly believed that He had, indeed, healed me, but now I did not know what to believe anymore. My trust in Him was being tested like never before. Yet, this was just the beginning; a long, dark, and lonely path lay ahead of me; eventually it would pull me to a place I did not want to go but did not have a choice. It was a path of isolation, fear, and torment—one where I had to trust God when I couldn't feel Him, to learn to walk by faith not by sight, to trust Him when everything in me told me to panic, to trust Him when opinion's of doctors contradicted what I knew to be true, to trust that He loved me even though I had to suffer for an unseen reason, and to trust that His grace was sufficient to get me through anything. There were times that I wanted to despair, but I was reminded daily just what it meant to persevere in the face of adversity.

During this time, I was working as a caregiver to a young woman who suffered from a rare, degenerative disease as well as dementia. Needing little assistance, the twenty-seven year old was living in her own apartment. I took the job as a companion/caregiver on Saturdays and spent those days taking her to the store or to the movies, hanging out with her, and making sure she remembered to take her medicine. She was so much fun to be with; I looked forward to being with her on the weekends. Her hair was strawberry blonde, her eyes the brightest of blue, and her laughter was contagious and made her whole body shake!

She loved movies, music, making art, and cute boys, giggling constantly if she saw one.

The progression of her disease was slow, and it took everything from her. Her need for care grew as she declined, and I eventually spent Monday through Friday of every week with her.

She was an amazing person and loved to make art. She would make beautiful weavings on a loom, but when she lost the use of her feet, she moved on to making art with clay. Over time as her disease progressed, that too, became hard for her hands to do anymore, so she moved on to painting. She did not let her decline stop her. Working with her showed me what it meant to push through no matter what. She showed me how to laugh when I wanted to cry, to look for new ways of doing things, to never stop dreaming, to never feel sorry for myself, and to keep the perspective that no matter how bad things got it could always be worse. Seeing what it took for her to live every day, I knew that no matter how much pain I was in I could get through it.

There were times when we would talk about heaven and how great it would be to be free of pain and suffering. We would sing about it, talk about it, read about it; we both looked forward to the day of being free. There was no cure for her disease; no one knew the prognosis for her because she had such a rare form of the condition, so all we could do was give her the best quality of life that we could, not knowing how long that would be. I was privileged to be a part of her life for ten years. She left the prison her body had become in March of 2010, free of her suffering once and for all.

My suffering paled in comparison to what this young woman went through, yet its grip on me was severe. As much as I would tell myself to suck it up and deal with it, sometimes I could, but then there were times I felt swallowed in darkness. I got to the point that I would hide it; I was tired of talking about it and didn't want to bring people down to where I was, so I acted like I was fine, but I wasn't. I was sinking in my thoughts and my emotions, and there was nothing I could do to stop it.

I was isolated from people, from relationships, and things seemed very dark.

During this time, I experienced something that I had not expected. I learned in that season that while things are dark there are songs in the night, but you never hear them until it is dark. I also learned that there is a sweetness that comes only through bitter heartache, there is a light that can only be seen in the dark, there is a comfort that is only felt after suffering, there is a supernatural strength that only comes when your own strength is completely gone, and there is a presence that is felt only when you are truly alone because no human can meet you there. I realized that God truly uses all things for our good and that a deep trust in Him is only formed when there is something greatly needed for Him to do for you, something you cannot do on your own.

I never would have understood how great His faithfulness is if I hadn't needed Him to do so much for me. I relied on Him for the strength to get up each day, the strength to push through the pain, the peace of mind to not panic when the pain was screaming at me to get help. I had to rely completely on Him for everything.

As I would turn to doctor after doctor, the Lord would show me that He was the One in control and He was the One I needed to trust. Repeated trips to the emergency room and never finding the problem, only concluding, "It is just your endometriosis; there is no cure." After hearing it over and over again, I began to believe that it could be the endometriosis, so I looked into the surgery in Oregon again. My insurance would only pay so much, so I had to have five thousand dollars before they would do the surgery. I knew there was no way we could come up with that much money, at least not for a very long time. All we could do was pray and trust that God knew what He was doing, but, over time, I had given up hope. Then the unthinkable happened!

A friend from church told us that God had put it on his heart to pay for me to get the surgery. He had even put it on someone else's heart to pay for my hotel for the week while I was recovering there. I was stunned and amazed at how quickly things changed! In a moment, the fog cleared; out of nowhere, God had provided the way and answered our prayers even greater than we had thought to ask. I was so happy at the possibility of putting an end to this pain, but there was something still bothering me. I still believed God had healed my endometriosis. I did not share this with anyone, but, the night before the surgery, I wrote in my journal:

May 20, 2005: "Thank you, Lord, for Your continued faithfulness; it never ends. Your peace has stayed with me through this whole ordeal. I have never had to be afraid; Your peace was always there. I have never felt alone, You were always there. You gave me a wonderful husband to help me through. Even though there is still a lot of unknown as far as what is wrong with me, I know I am in Your hands, and You know all things. You know the cause of my pain and if it will go away. My heart tells me that You healed my endo when I first came to You in July of 1999; my mind isn't sure. Please, if it be Your will, somehow show me or confirm it in my heart so I can truly give You the glory for it. Either way, the glory is Yours. I cannot thank You enough for how gracious and loving You have been to me. Looking back at the last time I went through this surgery and comparing it to this time is so amazingly different. I was so alone; the pain ran deeper than physical; it ran to the soul. I carried so much pain inside. The burden of my sin weighed so heavily upon me; I could not stand. I had no peace, only fear and isolation. When I came to You, You set me free. You lifted the burden of sin off of me and took it on Yourself. Is that when You healed my endo Lord? I believed it then; I believed it with all of my heart. My pain was gone from that day on, and I thanked and praised You for it. But when the pain came back, I thought maybe You never healed me but postponed the pain until I was stronger. Could it be that this pain was something completely different? I just don't know, but I guess I don't need to. I can only thank and praise You for Your tender love toward me. You have blessed me beyond anything I could have ever imagined. Salvation was more than I deserved, yet, You daily, compassionately, love me and care for me. Thank You, my dear sweet Father."

The surgery went well, and, after a few days of recovery, we met with the doctor. I will never forget him sitting down and telling me, "Well, we did not find any endometriosis, not even a cell of it." The words rang through my mind a few times before I could comprehend what he was saying...no endometriosis!

Instead, there were other problems like a blocked fallopian tube. They removed the blocked tube and my appendix as a precaution, but there was no endometriosis like there was when I had my first surgery.

God really did heal me on that summer day back in 1999 when I gave my life to Him. He took me on that long journey all the way to Oregon not for a cure from the pain but to show me how much He loved me, to show me He was faithful, to show me He was trustworthy, and, yes, to show me He had, indeed, healed me. Now, it wasn't just a feeling; I had medical proof!

After I recovered from the surgery, I thought things would get better, but they didn't. They actually got worse. The pain continued on my right side, sometimes so intense that I couldn't function. The next doctor suggested removing the ovary. Because I was so desperate, I had another surgery only six months after the surgery in Oregon.

As I lay on that operating table waiting for the anesthesia to kick in, I reminded myself of God's faithfulness through the whole thing. I knew at that moment that no matter what, He was with me and whatever lay ahead I would not face alone. I was scared, but I had peace.

After that surgery before I even had the chance to hope that it was over, I began producing blood filled cysts on the ovary I had left. They were so painful and excruciating that I ended up in the emergency room many times. When they would rupture, the blood would be in my abdomen and create such a distinctive pain that I learned to recognize it. There was nothing else like it. Each month that I produced one of these cysts, I risked it twisting and cutting off the circulation to the ovary, causing it to die and sending me instantly into menopause at the age of twenty-seven. I prayed desperately that God would spare me from that happening.

I had given up on a life without pain or having children. I decided that if it was God's will for me to suffer it was my lot to bear and I would take it, but menopause at such a young age seemed too much for me. I ended up at yet another doctor. This one was into naturopathy. She put me on a ton of different vitamins and supplements and somehow got the cysts to stop for two months!

A few months after not having a cyst I felt nauseous and dizzy, symptoms of pregnancy again, only this time I really was pregnant! Again, God showed me that He was capable of doing the impossible. He was able to do exceedingly abundantly above anything I could ever ask or think. His ways are so much better than mine, and He did more than I was even asking of Him. We were so surprised it was hard for us to be excited, fearing that at any moment it would end and we'd lose the baby. Yet, beyond our doubts and fears He gave us a beautiful, little girl named Grace, and, truly, it was because of His grace that we had her. Then to bless us beyond our measure to understand, I found out I was pregnant again when Grace was only eight months old. Another beautiful, baby girl was born to us, my Avery Joy.

Once again, God was not limited to the box mere men had created for Him. His will for our lives would not be stopped. He was able to even give me the fulfillment of dreams I was too afraid to dream, for fear of them not coming true. I was merely asking for an end to the pain, yet, He had something much greater for me, greater than I ever dared to ask. He would give me what was considered impossible, children of my own.

The sorrow of my heart had turned into unbelievable joy.

Chapter 15
Releasing Fear

"Fear not, for I am with you; be not dismayed for I am your God.
I will strengthen you, yes, I will help you,
I will uphold you with My righteous right hand."
Isaiah 41:10 (ESV)

July 2009, Grass Valley, California

HOW DID I GET HERE? I am holding the lifeless body of my nineteen month old daughter and watching helplessly as the ambulance passes my house, not sure where we were. The panic and fear of them not getting to her in time was more than I could take! I ran back into the house and called 911 again to tell them they had passed us, to tell them to please come quickly, and to please save my little girl! Helplessness consumed me. Again the dispatcher tried to reassure me that she just had a febrile seizure, something caused by a high fever. "Very common," she said, "Don't worry." Unconsoled, I was holding my unconscious daughter, and I knew she didn't have a fever. In fact, just a short time before, she had been fine, watching a cartoon and showing no signs of being sick.

A sunny, beautiful day in July of 2009, Aaron had left for work, and the girls and I were having a nice morning. When Grace had been only eight months old, God blessed us (and surprised us) with another pregnancy! Another beautiful daughter had been born. I had just finished nursing my little Avery and had put her in the bassinet in the living room. Grace was standing at the coffee table watching her favorite cartoon when she collapsed. I watched her little body go limp and fall to the ground. For a second, I thought she was playing, but I knew something was wrong; something was very wrong.

She was unresponsive as I called her name, picked her up, and cradled her in my arms. I set her on the couch and checked to see if she was choking, but she wasn't gasping for air. She was unconscious, and I couldn't get her to wake up. I grabbed the phone and dialed 911. She wasn't convulsing, so I didn't think it was a seizure and was surprised when the dispatcher said that it was probably a seizure caused by a fever spike. I kept feeling her forehead and her neck; she did not feel hot at all. It was as though eternity passed as I waited for the ambulance. I called Aaron at work, a call he would never forget.

The ambulance pulled in the driveway, and they came in quickly. They started examining her, then got her ready for transport as I grabbed her little car seat for the paramedics to take her. They asked me if I wanted to ride with them, but, because of having another infant, I had to say no and I would follow them after getting my other baby. The thought of being away from Grace for a moment and not knowing if she would make it struck immense fear in my heart. It was my only choice, so I ran into the house to get Avery and followed them. Aaron was meeting us at the hospital.

The doctors continued with the same idea as the dispatcher, that she just had a seizure from a fever spiking. No one was listening to me because she didn't have a fever. She finally started to wake up but seemed so groggy. I was so happy to see her bright, blue eyes looking at me. She smiled at me. My heart melted at the sight. She had the kind of smile that lit up her whole face, my sweet little girl. A short time before, I didn't know if I would ever get to see her smile again. So for me, it was a glimmer of hope—-a glimmer that shone brightly for a moment then quickly turned black.

Her bright, blue eyes looked off into some faraway place and locked into position. I couldn't get her to look at me. Her body got stiff as her eyes shut, then her whole body went limp. I started yelling for help, and immediately nurses and doctors were there tending to her. They surrounded her; I could only stand back and watch. They checked her and said she was seizing. The scene seemed so unnatural, her tiny, little body in that big bed surrounded by all those people. *How could this be happening?* They checked her pulse and her temperature; then I heard them say, "She doesn't have a fever." Finally, I knew they would believe me, although there was no satisfaction in finally being heard. The only feeling in that moment was fear. *Is my little girl about to die? What is wrong with her?*

They kept close watch on her until she eventually woke up again and cried for me. I had to hold her tightly as they tried to draw blood from her tiny, little veins as she screamed and screamed. I was so relieved when Aaron arrived; however, the way we looked at each other couldn't hide the fear that gripped us both...*Is she going to die? Our little surprise baby, our gift from God, the one who had brought so much joy to our lives...Are we about to lose her?*

Test after test was done, but there were no answers. After many hours, they told us to go home and follow up with her physician and, probably, a neurologist. *Go home?* That reality was terrifying as we had no answers as to why this happened and there was a very real possibility that it would just happen again. They said if it did happen again to come straight back into the emergency room. Going home had never been so scary, yet I longed for a sense of normalcy.

We all seemed relieved to be home again. I took a shower; Avery took another nap, but we could not take our eyes off Grace, afraid at any moment she would start seizing again. We fed her a small bowl of rice to start with after not being able to eat all day. We watched her as we fed her each bite; her sweet little countenance had returned as we pretended each small bite was being delivered by an airplane straight to her mouth. After each bite, she would smile and sign for "more". Once we gave her another bite, she would sign her own version of "thank you". I had taught her baby sign language when she was very little, and seeing her still able to do it brought a sense of assurance that she'd be okay.

Sadly, it was a sense that was short lived; she seized again. This time my husband was there, and this was the first one he had seen. She collapsed and made small convulsions with her little body. We grabbed Avery in her car seat still asleep, and I held Grace as Aaron drove us to the hospital. The drive was terrifying; the feeling of not being able to get there in time was causing fear to run through us like the blood pumping through our bodies. No matter how you tell yourself to hold it together, the constant pounding of the bad thoughts, telling you this is it, this will be the end of her life. I kept talking to her, but again she was lifeless; nothing I said to her would bring her back.

Aaron dropped me off at the entrance of the emergency room. Holding her in my arms, I ran in just to be stopped by the security guard at the door. He was telling me I couldn't go in. Panic and frustration took over as I yelled at him that I was told to come back if she had another seizure, that we had been there all day, and to let us in! Before I knew it, we were back in the same place but this time on a bed in the hallway since there were no empty rooms. Calm and collected, people doing their jobs walked past us as they worked. Everyone was busy with something to do, no one checked my little girl. I wanted to scream; I probably came close, but I had to wait. Finally, a doctor came and started to examine her. He was so calm and casual as he started to tell me about febrile seizures. Again, I explained the events of the day, trying to convince him that the child did not have a fever. Soon Aaron was there with Avery in tow in her little car seat. Again, my tiny, little girl was placed in a bed too big for her little body. Nurses were poking and prodding her trying to find a vein in her little arms. She seized again. Her whole body locked up; her eyes rolled into the back of her head, and thick white fluid was coming out of her mouth. Each seizure was getting worse! True terror struck my heart as I stood back, helpless to do anything. "Please, God, don't let her die. Help us!" I prayed over and over.

Once again the doctor on shift concluded that she did not have a fever. They decided to have us transferred to another hospital where there was a very good neurologist. Clearly something was very wrong with our daughter. Aaron and Avery went home to pack some things for us, while I rode in the ambulance with Grace. The same EMTs that came to my house that morning were the ones who drove us down. One of them was a kid from a youth group that Aaron and I had helped with before we had kids. There was great comfort in knowing one of them. We made small talk, and I knew he was praying for my little girl. I sat in the bed and held her in my arms the entire way. *Would this be the last time I get to hold her? Why would God give me this little miracle only to take her away?* Heartache and fear consumed me; the great unknown was overwhelming as I held her tightly, not wanting to let her go.

The next hospital was much bigger; and quicker, with test after test being done. The scariest was the spinal tap. They could not give her anything to stop the seizures until all the tests were completed. After that procedure, they gave her Dilantin, an anti-seizure medication. We were put in a room in the ICU ward with another family whose daughter was having seizures. There was no comfort in sharing a room with them as their poor little girl had seizures almost constantly, and her prognosis did not look good. Being so close to another family that was living through the same horror seemed to confirm the fear that was already attacking our thoughts. *Will we ever have our little girl back?*

As Grace woke up from the anesthesia, she cried and cried. She wouldn't hold still; it was like she was trying to crawl out of her own skin! We would hold her, and she would calm down for a few seconds, then start flailing and arching her back. My arms ached trying to hold her. Aaron and I looked at each other, terrified that somehow we had permanently damaged our little girl. *What happened to her?* She was inconsolable, and holding her was so hard that we had to take turns every ten minutes or so. We walked up and down the halls trying to soothe her, trying not to disturb the other poor people in ICU who were attempting to sleep. It was the longest night of my life. At one point, they gave her a sedative. She finally rested in the metal crib in our room. After only an hour, she woke up screaming and crying. The entire night was spent pacing the halls, holding her, trying to help her but unable to. All night I prayed as I battled the thoughts that God didn't really love us. Repeatedly I begged Him to heal my little girl. The doctor told us that she may have had an allergic reaction to the anti-seizure medicine and, if so, that would pass in twenty-four hours and she should get better. After keeping everyone up the entire night, they gave us our own room.

Finally, the effects seemed to wear off, and she started to calm down. However, the next day came with yet another seizure. This time her lips turned blue. The neurologist was there; he was so calm and collected I just wanted to scream, "Make it stop!" I thought for sure that she was going to die. It was Aaron's thirtieth birthday, July 16th, 2009, and our little girl was going to die. The stress and the up and down of fear and emotions after seven seizures in a twenty-four-hour-period were so overwhelming that it seemed more than I could take but somehow had to. People from church came and brought us food. They would hold Avery for us, take my clothes home and wash them, pray with us, and visit with us. Their care provided a level of sanity with me in a place that was like a slow torture of my heart and mind.

The room in the ICU was so small I had to sleep in a chair next to Grace's crib. Since there was nowhere for Aaron to sleep they let him stay in a place for families with sick kids near the hospital. The nurses wheeled in a toy wagon from the toy room down the hall so Avery would have a place near me to sleep in. At only three months old she fit perfectly in the wagon and was a precious sight to see. Her sweet, little face would look at me and smile at moments when I wanted to fall apart; it even made me smile at a time when joy felt impossible. Seeing Grace suffer broke my heart and brought such sorrow every time

I looked at her. So when I saw Avery's sweet, toothless, baby smile, it softened the fear that had taken residence in my heart; I truly needed her just as much as she needed me. She was a light in my darkness.

Every day that passed felt like three, but the day finally came when they believed we could go home. A different anti-seizure medication they had given her had stopped the seizures for several days. They came to the conclusion that the cause of it all was from the birthing process. She had had a very difficult birth; it really was the only trauma she had ever experienced in her short life. After a very long delivery and her getting stuck in the birth canal, they had used the forceps to help get her out. She was born with a black eye and still has a little scar from it just below her eye. They said that it could have caused damage and then scarring to her brain. As her brain grew, the scarring aggravated it and caused seizures. It seemed impossible that this could happen such a long time after her birth, but the neurologist said it was not uncommon to not have seizures from a brain trauma for one to five years after the incident as it could take that long to heal from it. One to five years sounded like forever, but he assured us that as long as we didn't notice any developmental problems as she grew she should be all right.

Leaving the hospital was such a relief after almost a week there, but a heavy sense of fear and responsibility came with it. She could have a seizure anytime. *Could I ever take my eyes off her? What if she had one when I was asleep or near water?* We had an emergency syringe that contained a special medicine to be given if she had multiple seizures in a short time that I had to carry everywhere. Life completely changed for us; there was no going back to "normal" once we were home. There had to be a new normal, but it eluded us for quite some time. Even our sense of time changed. For us, everything was marked by the day of the seizures; everything was either before or after seizures. Although Grace had recovered from the allergic reaction she had experienced, there were significant changes in her. Her new medicine brought a whole host of side effects with it (like depression and suicidal tendencies) ones that were hard to recognize in an almost two year old. She seemed to be more fearful of many things and stopped doing things she used to like. She was more afraid of people and very clingy; she wouldn't go on a slide or a swing at the park. My once social, sweet, little baby became very shy and afraid of the world around her. I had no idea what the future held for her, no idea if she would make it, no idea how long we would have her in our lives.

It was at this time that I realized just how fragile life really is. That sweet little girl was truly on loan to us from God, and my uncertainty about her future was actually the reality that we all face everyday but try not to think about. We never know how much time we have; we never know what the future holds for us here on earth, when things take such a drastic change that we can never go back. I knew when I had her that she was such a gift to us. Her name was a reminder that He was the one who gave her to us in the first place. It really took experiencing a loss of all control to realize I never had control in the first place. I did not create her life nor was I able to keep it. I had to completely trust in the One who did create her life, the One who had the power to keep it, the One who could heal her, the One who could see her when she slept each night, the One who knew all things—-even the number of her days. I had to trust completely in His goodness and love, even if it meant submitting to His will to take her to heaven. I understood His will was greater than mine and His purposes much higher than mine. I discovered quickly that it was easier to trust God with my life than it was to trust Him with the life of my child, but it was a necessary lesson because her life was in His hands; she belonged to Him not us. In that challenging season, I saw Him be faithful to us time and time again. My daughter grew and did not have any developmental problems. After a year without a seizure, it was time to slowly wean her off the medicine for another year. She continued to do well and slowly overcame her fears with the help of a fearless, little sister leading the way down steep slides head first and over any other obstacle that crossed her path.

When I look at the precious person she is today, God's Grace is revealed. I see His great love for us and how He used that struggle for our good and His glory. A faith that cannot be tested is no faith at all; it is just lip service. I see that no matter how we feel in a situation the outcome belongs to God, and He is good. He does good, and He does love us even when we cannot feel it.

Chapter 16
Relentless Mercy

"Let my prayer come before You; incline Your ear to my cry.
For my soul is full of troubles, and my life draws near to the grave."
Psalm 88:2-3 (NKJV)

November 2013, Grass Valley California

HOW DID I GET HERE? Standing in front of my house holding the remains of my brother in a box. I trembled at the thought of it, so I held the box even tighter, knowing that all that was left of him was now in my shaking hands.

Ashes! Matt's life was nothing but ashes now—-ashes they shipped to my house in the mail. My thoughts were screaming at me. How is this even possible? This can't be real. Dear God, help me wake up; this cannot be real! How did it come to this? This is permanent, Lord; he can't come back. This is final. Then a quiet whisper spoke to my heart, "No, Joy, this is not permanent; this life is temporary. Where he is now is what's permanent; that lasts forever."

I will never forget how gracious God was with my brother. No matter what he did or how far he would drift, God would always draw him back. The Lord would always provide for Matt whenever he would come to his senses and return to Him. I saw him go from rags to Jesus many times; each time God did great things for him and moved many mountains on his behalf.

One of those times, God had miraculously provided the money for Matt to go to a Christian rehabilitation facility when he had been strung out on drugs and was homeless. He was there at the time when I was going to get married. Matt wasn't able to come to the wedding because he was in a rehabilitation program. I did want Matt's blessing, and, surprisingly, when I called him and told him whom I was marrying, he sounded surprised and said, "Aaron? Really? I know that guy; he is the nicest guy I have ever met. I am happy for you, Joy." I was so shocked! I had expected my brother to question me and threaten to kill Aaron if he hurt me, but, instead, he knew him and approved! What I didn't know at the time, and didn't find out for many years later, was that Aaron had been the young man who used to pick up my brother from a different drug rehab and take him to church; he was the one who prayed with my brother to receive Christ as his Savior. I married him not knowing that, and Aaron was not the kind of guy to brag about things that God did through him, so I didn't find out for years! However, the Lord did know. He had designed it that way for a purpose.

Matt always had great respect for my husband, and my husband always had great compassion for Matt. Because of it, Matt never tried to take advantage of us nor continually borrow from us and not pay it back. Nor did he ever steal from us like he did other family members when his addictions got bad. He only would ask for help when he needed it and was ready to get off drugs because he knew we would never support his drug use. We knew that the key to freedom from addictions was in the hands of the Saviour and Matt's surrendering to Him was the only way to have a new life. My brother knew it, too, and would only come to us when he was ready to surrender. For years I had been so full of hope that God was going to change him and set him free once and for all.

I saw God do great things in him many times. In fact, every time he would finally surrender. I saw God restore him every time, blessed with all of his needs taken care of, his marriage restored, and then given two beautiful children. Each time, I would witness healing, healing in his mind and physical body, provision of good jobs and places to live. Matt would be truly taken care of, yet somehow, every time, when things were good, something would draw him back. It always started with small compromises, a beer or a joint. Unfortunately, it never ended there; methamphetamines always followed, always pulled him farther and farther away. I saw him lose everything many times, and with each time the addictions grew stronger and more fierce. Each relapse took him to another whole level and made it harder and harder to come out, costing him more and more each time. Each plunge into darkness carried the consequences of guilt and shame of things he did while using, making it harder to live with the guilt. The guilt and shame drove him to use more drugs just to escape the feelings, but the drugs created more things of which to be ashamed. A vicious vortex consumed all that was good in his life until there was nothing left. Sadly, he couldn't feel good high, and he couldn't feel good sober. There was no escape, and death looked better than life to him.

He was in the Wayne Brown Correctional Facility in February of 2013 where he first tried to hang himself. The noose he had made with his clothes broke, and he landed hard on the cement, hurting his leg. He said the guards saw him and laughed. Broken, ashamed, and at the end of himself, he called me and begged for help. "I have lost everything, Joy; I have nothing left. Please help me."

How many rock bottoms can a person hit? I will never know; I now know that the bottom can always go lower than you ever expect. I confess that my heart was hardened toward Matt; walls had been erected around my heart to protect it, to guard it against the pain of seeing him go back time and time again and to prevent the slow torture of watching the brother I loved so much self destruct.

Admittingly, at first I didn't want to help him again; it never seemed to help anyway. Too many times I had helped him, only for him to bail out. He had burned every bridge, left every program, and destroyed every relationship in the family. I was the only one left in the family who was still talking to him. Even my husband had grown tired of helping him. Yet something was pulling on my heart; it weighed heavily upon me. I couldn't ignore it. I prayed, and I prayed; I asked others to pray. It continued as a month passed. The Lord was telling me it was time to help him again. I started looking into programs again; then doors began to open, and I knew it was the Lord. I put fleeces before the Lord so as not to step outside His will; I didn't want to get in the way of what He was doing. Time and time again He answered and confirmed that it was time to help my brother again. I knew he was at the point of death.

When I went to see him at the jail, there was a deep darkness in his eyes; he couldn't even smile, and he looked like he was dying. Frightened and paranoid, he was talking about these people who were after him because he witnessed something. Matt spoke of these people who were going to torture him and kill him and he had to get out of town. Through his descriptions of everything, I could tell they were hallucinations and not based in reality. It seemed as though every time he got high, his brain would store the hallucinations as memory, and each high would build upon it until he had many memories of things that never even happened. However, there was no convincing him. Miraculously, we were able to get him to a Christian, sober living apartment in Huntington Beach the morning he got out of jail. He made it down there and started doing well again. It wasn't easy because there were many obstacles to overcome, yet he seemed determined to do it, determined to make it, determined that one day he would be clean and would get to see his kids again. He found a good church, got baptized again, and saw God start to move in his life again, taking care of his daily needs one by one. Excitement began to bud and take bloom. This was it; my brother was finally going to be set free! He told me in an email, "I can't explain how much happens in a day, spiritually, mentally. I love you guys. God is good."

After six weeks of him doing well and not bailing out of the program, I felt such anticipation at the great things that were going to happen. I was beyond shocked when I got a call on a Sunday from him, "Joy, they are after me. They are going to kill me, Joy; they have found me. They are going to rape me, torture me, and kill me. I have to kill myself; I have no other choice!" I could tell by the sound of his voice he was high. With anger swelling in my throat, I tried to stay calm as I responded, "Did you get high again?"

He was quiet for a moment, then said, "Yes."

"Why, Matt? Why would you do this? Why would you throw it all away? His answer was simple, "I don't know why I did. I just felt like using it, so I did." His simple answer played in my mind over and over. I was so angry. How could he do it? He had gotten kicked out the moment the home found out he was high and had been wandering the streets for hours not knowing where to go or what to do, convinced he could see "them" following him. In his attempt to hide from "them" he went to a hospital. His delusions were so severe he believed the nurses were in on it and going to let "them" know where he was. He truly thought it was only a matter of time until "they" got him. He talked about killing himself; it was the only way out. He was going to walk out onto the highway into oncoming traffic and end it. Nothing I said seemed to help. I prayed with him and begged him not to hurt himself or anyone else. He said he had to go, and we hung up. The next day, he called me from a mental hospital. He had checked himself there so he wouldn't kill himself and "they" wouldn't get him. He whispered into the phone, "Joy, this place is surrounded; the police are in on it, so are the nurses. They are going to have me killed."

I tried to reason with him. "Matt, why would people risk their lives, their families, and their careers to have you killed? What have you ever done besides hurt yourself?" For an hour I talked to him, and tried to reason with him, trying to explain the hallucinations, the importance of his life, how he needed to live for his kids, and how God could help him. Trying to instill hope, I shared that God was bigger than his problems and could protect him. I prayed with him again, begging him not to give up, to keep fighting, and to let the drug wear off. Two days later, he called me crying, "Joy, I wish you would believe me."

I told him, "I do believe you, Matt. It is real; Satan is trying to kill you. He wants you to commit suicide; he is after you. The moment you got high you gave him control, and he is trying to destroy you." Later on that afternoon when I called, he was asleep, so we didn't talk. That night at church was a worship and prayer service. I remember going in there so heavy with the battle my brother was facing. I prayed for him that night, begging God to break the chains that held him, to set him free once and for all. That was the night before Halloween 2013, and everything felt so dark, so demonic. I could feel the spiritual battle taking place like never before. The whole church body prayed with me, interceding for him; I knew things were going to happen, and they did. Chains were broken then; my prayers were answered—-but not the way I had expected or hoped.

The next day the phones at the mental hospital didn't work, so it wasn't until the following day, Friday, that we talked again. He sounded good. I thought maybe the drugs had finally worn off because he did not mention "them". He asked me for the phone number to the sober living apartments so he could get his stuff. I gave it to him then asked him if he was okay. He said, "Yes." I felt so relieved; really believing the drugs had finally worn off. That night at 10:30 PM, I got a call from the mental hospital. My brother had hanged himself in the shower; they had done CPR and gotten his heart going again, but he was on his way to the emergency room. When I called the ER, they said he had not arrived yet and to call back in half an hour. It was the longest half hour of my life. I was home alone with my girls; Aaron had gone camping, and the girls and I were watching a movie. *I was in shock. He really did it, but he is not going to die. He can't! It can't end like this! This was just an attempt. They stopped him right? He will be fine. He will regret it, and everything will be fine. It has to be!* When I finally got in touch with the ER, they said he had been stabilized but that they were going to cool down his body to prevent brain damage and that after twenty-four hours they would rewarm him and that they would know more at that point. My friend came over, helped me get the kids to bed, and prayed with me.

After she left, I sat on my couch and picked up my Bible, searching for some comfort, something from the Lord to help me in this dark and lonely moment, something to hold on to. Instinctively, I turned to the book of Psalms. Many times I had found comfort within those pages, comfort from the struggles of others that ended with rejoicing and praising God for His great deliverances. Surely, tonight would be the same; surely, He would encourage me that way again. I felt strongly drawn to Psalm 88. I didn't remember that one, but it started in pain and ended there. There was no rejoicing, no praise like all the other Psalms ended. It brought me no comfort; I didn't understand until I realized it was a clear picture of the torment through which my brother had been—-no doubt how he felt right up until the moment he did it. The Lord was showing me a glimpse of Matt's despair, his isolation, and his anguish because one day it would bring comfort knowing his suffering was over; it just wasn't comfort to me then.

I had to call my mom to tell her. Matt had me down as his emergency contact, so they would only talk to me. The anticipation of calling her was far worse than the reality. She was so calm, almost like she knew this day would come. It seemed almost inevitable the chaos of addictions couldn't last forever, that one day it would end.

From that moment on, a heaviness loomed over my every thought and an uneasiness in the pit of my stomach. I needed to see him; I needed to be near him. I felt so anxious not knowing; there were so many unknowns. *Would he be a vegetable? Would he recover and regret the suicide attempt like so many do who survive? Would he recover, then do it again? Would I have to make the decision to take him off life support?* God alone knew the answers to all the unknowns. I had to wait and trust.

When they warmed his body, he started having seizures. They said it did not look good and that we needed to come down. Our church paid for my mom and me to fly down to Huntington Beach to be with him. My youngest brother Jonathan was living in Santa Cruz at the time and drove down to the airport and picked us up. I could not get there fast enough! Walking into the room where my brother was in the ICU brought such a surprising sense of relief to have finally made it.

There he was; it was really Matt, and we were finally there to be with him! He looked good, as crazy as that sounds. He looked so strong and healthy even though he was hooked up to all sorts of machines. I touched his hand; it felt stiff and colder than I expected, but he looked very much alive. I spoke to him and let him know we were there, that he wasn't alone. We prayed over him, trusting that whatever the outcome, God was good and that his life and his eternal soul were in His hands.

After getting some food, we went to our hotel that night not knowing what the days ahead would hold, not knowing the outcome, only knowing and sensing that we were on an incredible, life changing journey. We began the journey knowing that many decisions lay before us; yet, while we thought we were making the decisions and doing things on our own, we really were just along for the ride. The decisions had already been made by God; they actually weren't ours to make anyway. The course had been set, and we embarked on a path that was already prepared for us to walk. We only needed to follow it.

The doctors had no answers for us. They said it might take weeks to know, but I knew in my heart it wouldn't. Strangely, our return flight home would be in four days. While I prepared myself for needing to come back, I knew somehow it would all be done by then, and it was. After spending the day at the hospital, we went to the sober living apartments where he had been staying and broke the news to them. They were shocked; they said they told him he would have been allowed to come back in fourteen days. They let us get his stuff. As we were looking through trash bags of my brother's belongings, I found a note that I had written to him when he left. It was too much, and I broke down as I realized all that was left of his life was in these trash bags. *How is this possible?*

The next day after spending time at the hospital, my youngest brother asked us if we wanted to go to the mental hospital. I was so glad he had asked. I so badly wanted to see it for myself but didn't want to make anyone else feel like they had to. We all agreed, and we went.

At the mental hospital, they took us into a room and sat down with us to talk, to see how he was, and to check how we were. I could sense that they were probably afraid that we would sue them or blame them for what had happened. The director of the place started the conversation by informing us that in the forty years they had been in operation, no one had ever hanged himself there before. *Leave it to Matt to do what had never been done.* She talked about how she understood what we were going through, that her husband was bipolar. She looked at me and said, "I know exactly how you feel." Those words were like pouring salt on an open wound. *How could she know exactly how I felt? Was her husband on life support after hanging himself in her hospital?* The anger inside me was heating up; I could feel it rising to the surface, burning in my face. I wanted to scream at her, at all of them: *He came here so he wouldn't take his life! Why was he able to do it? Why didn't you stop him?*

The woman sitting across from me must have sensed the turmoil inside me. Looking at me she said, "You are his sister. He talked about you. I read it in his files. You were a great source of comfort to him." Those words were like cool water washing over me. *He knew; he knew I loved him. He knew I wanted him to live.* The anger subsided momentarily and was replaced with the heartache of his choice...his choice.

We asked if we could see where he did it; they said they could show us a room like it. It was an old hospital that had been redone and served a new purpose for the mentally ill. We followed her down the hallway as she told us what different areas were. She showed us his bedroom, then took us into a bathroom that was directly off the hallway and required a key to get into. It was a small room tiled from floor to ceiling. The entire room was the shower. She pointed to the vents on the ceiling. A square of tiny square holes was all that it was but now covered with a screen, something in place after what he had done. They had never thought anyone could fit a noose through the tiny squares. I don't even know how he did it. When she saw how calm we were, she said, "This is the room he did it in." We already knew. Why was there comfort in seeing it? I needed to know. I had to; I needed to see it. My dark imaginations were far worse than the reality, and I needed to know where his last, conscious moments were spent. A piece of the strange puzzle was now in place, and I was aware of how desperately he wanted to end it, how hard he worked to make it happen, how genius he had to be to pull it off, and how determined he was to even have to lift his legs because of the height of the ceiling. Nothing was going to stop him once the decision had been made.

By facing our fears and going to that place, we were able to get his Bible. It was like receiving a gift he had left behind. He had underlined verses about fighting to live. Underlined heavily was Psalm 118:17 " I will not die, but live, and declare the works of the Lord." He had wanted to live, but he couldn't live like that anymore. They said the night he had hung himself he was in his bedroom on his knees praying with his Bible open on the bed. He seemed fine later on when he asked to take a shower. He was on five-minute checks. So, five minutes later when the staff member knocked on the door and he didn't answer, the orderly went to go look for him somewhere else, assuming he had left the shower. Being unable to find him, the employee went back, unlocked the door and found him, then immediately did CPR. My heart was grieved for the staff member who had found him. That night will forever be engraved in his mind, forever haunting him of how he could've handled it differently. He probably blames himself for not opening that door first thing. At first, I blamed the staff, too, but then I remembered that God is sovereign. If He had wanted that door opened at that moment, it would have been. The outcome had been in His hands, no one else's.

When we went back to the hospital, Matt's situation had declined. I sat by his bedside with my hand on his arm. He was warm now, even a little hot as infection had set in. Suddenly his arm started to move! My heart jumped, and for a moment I thought he had awakened. For a moment I thought the nightmare would be over and my brother would live, but he was having seizures. Despite the medicines they were giving him to stop them, he was still seizing. The brain damage was too much; he was not going to make it. Their question to us became how long did we want to prolong it. The decision was made to take him off life support. I had pictured being with him to the end, but they said it could be very hard, very traumatic. Because we wanted to donate his organs, they said the window of opportunity would be small to get them out successfully.

We said our goodbyes that night on November 6, 2013. My mom and Jonathan each spoke to him, saying their goodbyes, but I couldn't speak. The words wouldn't come out; I couldn't say anything at all. I was crushed beyond words. *What could I possibly say now?* When I looked at him that last time, I could see he was already gone. He didn't look alive anymore like he had that first day we visited him; he looked like a body, an empty shell. He wasn't there; he was already gone.

That night we went to the church he had been attending for their mid-week service. We got to meet the people who had been ministering to him, who had helped him. It was an amazing feeling and healing experience to be there with them. During the worship service, there was a song that deeply spoke to me. It flooded my heart with comfort and understanding that I can't explain. The lyrics said, "Though the sorrow may last for the night, His joy comes with the morning; His love never fails." As it turned out, that was the exact moment they were taking my brother off life support, the very moments his heart stopped beating. The lyrics spoke truth to me. Night, indeed, had come into my life at that moment, and sorrow came with it, sorrow like I had never experienced before.

The next day was a whirlwind, the day of our flight home but also the day we had to make arrangements for Matt's remains. Somehow we were able to do it all in the small window of time that we had. We took care of everything we had to do at the hospital. We went to social services to make financial arrangements for his cremation, to the funeral home providing the service, back to the hotel, and finally to the airport. God directed our steps; He helped us get the information we needed every moment we needed it. Everything fell into place as we followed the path that laid before us. It was a dark path, but we were not alone. Although we thought we were making decisions, they had already been made for us. On that trip I saw God's great grace one more time for my brother. I realized that it was God's mercy that my brother died. He knew the shame and the torment that he was in; He knew that the drugs had defeated him and that he was not going to have victory over them, so in His grace and His mercy, He took him home. I believe He did it the night my brother hanged himself, November 1, 2013. His shell was left for us; his spirit was already gone. Because of how it happened, we had the chance to see him again, to know for certain that it was Matt, to go on the journey to see where he had been, to put the puzzle pieces together, to understand what happened, and to say goodbye.

Now, there was no doubt in my mind that the ashes in my hands really did belong to my brother. They were his remains, but they were only the remains of his shell. His spirit is alive and well in the presence of our Savior. Because of the great sacrifice of Jesus, who died for all sin, I will get to see my brother again. Matt made many bad choices in his life, but his choice to trust Christ for his salvation was the single greatest choice he ever made. Christ's sacrifice was enough. Matt has entered into eternity because of God's grace, because Jesus died to set the captives free, and his captivity was finally over.

Chapter 17
My Guide in the
Valley of the Shadow

"But He said to me, "My grace is sufficient for you,
for My power is made perfect in weakness."
Therefore I will rather boast all the more gladly of my weaknesses,
so that the power of Christ may rest upon me."
2 Corinthians 12:9 (ESV)

July 2014, Grass Valley, California

HOW DID I GET HERE? I am bleeding internally. I know I am dying. Hunched over in intense pain, I stood by my bed, trying to will myself to ignore it, to somehow push through it. I needed to be well and I needed to be strong. Both of Matt's kids were staying with me that weekend for the first time since his death. I wanted to be with them. I needed it; I desperately needed to feel connected to him, somehow, because he had been ripped from my heart and my life, and I longed to have something of him near me, no matter how much it hurt me to see him in their eyes. A soft voice kept repeating in my mind, "Go to the hospital; go now." I fell to my knees and prayed, begging for relief or for wisdom on what to do. "Go to the hospital; go now," repeated again and again. I stood up, sat on the bed, and called my husband. I knew what I needed to do. I had to go. When I told my husband I needed to go back to the emergency room, he was a little hesitant and said, "Are you sure? What if they just send you home again? We have been there so much already." It was true; I had already been there two other times that week and had been sent home each time. I had been having severe abdominal pain for two weeks before I even went to the

ER the first time. I told the doctor what was going on and that I felt like there was blood in my abdomen because it was something I had experienced many times before and knew that distinct type of pain. He looked at me and said, "If you had blood in your abdomen you would be in a lot more pain." Surprisingly, he must not have realized that I was sitting in the ER because I was in a lot of pain! Determining that I probably had a miscarriage or something, he blew me off and wanted to send me home. I knew something was wrong and asked him if we could at least do an ultrasound; he reluctantly agreed. About four hours later, he came into the room with the results. "You do have blood in your abdomen! Looks like you have a large cyst on your ovary, too. Do you want something for the pain?" I looked at my best friend who had been patiently waiting with me all day, and our eyes said the words we were thinking. So *nice to finally be heard; too bad it took this long!*

Later that week, I went to my doctor for a follow-up appointment. He, too, confirmed the hospital's results and said it would take a few days but my body would absorb the cyst and the blood in my abdomen, but if for some reason the pain got worse to go back in. They assured me everything would be just fine. A few days later, things were worse; something felt terribly wrong. It was not fine. I went back to the ER and was treated much differently. No one blew me off, and they got me a bed right away. They immediately gave me something for the pain and started running tests. (It probably helped that my friend from church was working in the ER that day, too.) They decided to do a CT scan to see what was going on. I was wheeled into the room, but, just before they put the IV with the dye in, I begged them to let me use the bathroom first (because I couldn't hold it much longer). So I got up and went, but when I came out of the restroom, they informed me that they had gotten a call from the ER doctor saying they could not do the scan. It was a good thing that they had not put in the dye.

Not knowing what in the world was happening, I was wheeled back to my bed in the emergency department. The doctor came in and said,

"Your tests came back positive for pregnancy; we can't do a CT scan while you're pregnant." *Pregnant?* I never expected him to say that. I had just had a test the last time I was in there a few days ago. How was this possible? My head was spinning. It wasn't that I didn't want to be pregnant. I had been praying for a third child for a while.

Two months before this ordeal, I had thought I was pregnant. I was late in my cycle, dizzy, nauseous, and had even gotten excited at the possibility, but only my best friend knew about it because I wasn't sure. My heart desperately wanted to feel joy again. I thought maybe a new baby would bring happiness to me, some warmth and light in my life after being in the painful dark for the past nine months since my brother's death. When I got my period, the short-lived fantasy was crushed, and I had to let it all go. Only my period never really stopped, and I had been spotting ever since, followed by horrible and intense pain for weeks. The pieces all started to come together. I felt sick; I didn't feel joy. Something was wrong, very wrong. I had been pregnant before, but I had never felt like this.

Pulling me from my thoughts and back to reality, the doctor said, "We do not know if the baby is in the uterus or not. It could be a tubal pregnancy, but it is too early to tell. We will wait a few days then try to do an ultrasound to see where it is. Go home, rest, and come back if it gets worse."

The following day was going to be the first time I had Matt's kids come stay with me since his death. They were living out of town and this was finally my chance to be with them. Despite my reservations because of my health, l had them come anyway. I thought it would be fine. Knowing I had a high pain tolerance, I figured that I could just push through it. I wanted to see them. I wanted to be near them, near to him somehow. I could see him when I looked at them. Sometimes great sorrow filled me when I saw him reflected in their faces; other times it was anger. *How could he have done it? How could he leave them?*

The pain I had felt every moment since his death was far greater than the pain I felt in my abdomen.

So many feelings rushed through me that weekend: anger, sorrow, emptiness, regret, pain. I couldn't stop thinking about him; I couldn't enjoy anything. Every smile was forced; every action took all my strength. There was a heaviness that never went away. It kept me a prisoner trapped within my thoughts and memories. I could hear his voice, our last conversations, playing in my mind over and over again. *Why couldn't I have talked him out of it? What else should I have said? What else could I have done? Why did it have to end like this?* The burden of being the last to talk to him was given to me; I didn't understand it. I could only doubt and question everything I had chosen to say in those moments. The importance of my words, of any of our words, was too heavy a burden to think of in light of his death, yet it was mine to carry. I was alone in that dark place where no human could follow me and no one could understand what was happening in my mind. Words could never explain it nor allow someone to enter it with me. The pain was consuming me, and I could only cry out to the Lord to keep my face above water because I was truly drowning in sorrow.

After spending the weekend with my niece and nephew, I did not feel closer to Matt. Instead, I felt angry that he had chosen to leave and hurt that the pain he had been in was so great that he had left the way that he did. I knew how much he had loved his children, and the thought of how great his sorrow and shame had been for him to think that they would be better off without him was devastating and overwhelming.

Meanwhile, my body was getting worse every hour. It seemed easier to ignore because of the emotional pain I was in, but on Sunday after church it changed. I couldn't ignore it any longer. I was dying; I could feel it. Life felt like it was draining out of me. It had only been nine months since my brother's death. *Would I die now, too?* I felt like I was already dead anyway, emotionally, spiritually, and, now finally, physically. I felt so broken and unfixable inside. My painful existence seemed like it couldn't continue. Such a large part of me died with my brother. It had left a gaping hole that felt like it was bleeding uncontrollably and that nothing could stop it. The amount of strength it took everyday just to do the daily things of being a wife, mother, and friend was too much. Everything was more than I could handle. In a way, I longed for it all to be over.

My husband found people to watch the kids and took me to the ER again. This time there was a real urgency within the staff, and the doctor came in quickly. They wanted to know the last time I ate because they wanted to operate. Surprisingly, I had forgotten to eat lunch that day (something very unusual for me), so they were going to do it within the hour. As I looked at my husband, I could see the fear in his eyes without him even speaking. Although I longed for an end to my pain, I didn't want my husband and kids to go through anything like what I was feeling, to have to lose their mom or my husband to lose his spouse. I could imagine how much that would hurt them. Finally, my eyes were off me and my pain, and I thought of them. *Please, God, don't let me die now.*

Once again I was wheeled into a cold, bright, sterile operating room. There were people busy making preparations and moving instruments into place until one by one they came around to where I was lying having finished their tasks. My heart was pounding uncontrollably; tears were flowing down my cheeks; fear was trying to lay hold of me, to take me as a prisoner. *You are going to die!* The thoughts in my mind kept screaming at me. *This is it! You are done, you will die now!* The people around me stood there looking at me as the anesthesiologist explained how they would count down until I was asleep. My heart continued to race, but in my mind I kept repeating one thing over and over again, *"Lord, my life is in your hands; my life is in your hands."* No matter the outcome, I knew I was in the hands of the Creator. I would not leave this earth a moment too soon or a moment too late; my life belonged to the One who had made it, and no one or no thing could take it from Him. That alone gave me peace as I drifted into unconsciousness.

The surgery revealed that the pregnancy was, in fact, a tubal one and that I had been bleeding internally from it rupturing. While the surgery was able to stop the bleeding and save my life, it did not fix what was broken in my heart—that bleeding couldn't be repaired as easily. Yet, my faithful and loving Father was working on it. He wouldn't leave me in that condition just as the surgeon wouldn't leave me bleeding internally. The Great Physician was the only One who could repair the damage that had been done from the heartbreak of losing my brother and use it for something far greater than I. Although there are some pains that last a lifetime and will only be healed in heaven, the healing will come and there will be beauty coming from the ashes, even in this life. The worst things, the hardest things, the painful and the ugliest things can be used for good when given to the Lord.

After the surgery, I was physically, emotionally, and mentally broken. I was finished; I felt like I had nothing left. Thankfully though, where our strength ends God's begins, and where we give up and surrender is where God can really begin to rebuild! My entire life changed that year. I hadn't wanted it to. I hadn't asked for it, but change was unavoidable. It crashed on me when I wasn't looking and took all that I knew. There was no going back. I would never be the same person I was before my brother died. My only option was to move forward and to allow God to have His way with me, to make me into something new, to do something with the pain, to make something of value out of my brokenness, and to, hopefully, help me survive it all. Through that experience, God was revealing Himself to me daily. He walked me through a darkness that seemed to have no end, but thankfully it did. He gave me strength when I had none. In my quiet moments of despair, He showed me that He knew what I was feeling and that, although no one else knew what was happening in my heart and mind, He did know and I wasn't alone. I found out that He is truly intimate with us and is a God of secrets, not that He keeps secrets from us but that we can share secrets with Him and Him alone. We had many secrets together during this time, things that no one else knew about, so that He could encourage me in ways that no one else could.

In the moments when I was trying to hold it all together outwardly so no one would know the pain I was in, He would meet me there because He was the only one who even knew where I really was. We had secret songs together, songs that meant so much to me, songs that spoke to me in dark moments that only He knew about.

Many times I would try to go about my life as though things were normal, and I would find myself suddenly sinking in sorrow and grief when a song, our song, would come on the radio in that moment and remind me that He knew. He knew what I was thinking. He knew what I was feeling in that isolated moment of pain, and I wasn't alone. We had secret Scriptures that spoke to my heart exactly where I was, and He would remind me of them when I wanted to despair. Through His Word, He was regularly reminding me that this life was not my home, that someday I would be there, that someday I would see my brother again, and that someday the wrong things would be made right. There were so many precious moments that shine brightly in my memory of those dark days, so many times He would do things to draw me out of the pain and remind me how great He is.

I especially have to laugh when I think about a place called John's Incredible Pizza. A place that should have been fun and exciting with my kids became a dark and painful place for me until the Lord turned it all around. On Saturday, November 2, 2013, we were invited to a birthday party for a friend at the fun arcade with rides and prizes and, of course, pizza! Only, on November 1, 2013, at 10:30 PM, I got the call about my brother. I had no idea at that point if he would make it or not. I only knew he was on life support. My husband was out of town camping, so it was just the girls and I. They had been looking forward to this party, so I had decided to go anyway since there was nothing I could do about my brother at that moment and the thought of sitting at home sounded like pure torture. I walked around that place like a zombie. My kids ran around laughing and having fun, but, being consumed in the many thoughts and fears about my brother's fate, I did not enjoy a moment of it.

After a long year of grief, the following fall we were invited to a birthday party at John's Incredible Pizza again! Walking into the building immediately brought back the memories of the day after getting the phone call, that day that forever changed my life. Flashbacks brought every level of pain back into my mind, and once again I was like a zombie walking through a children's arcade. This time I knew the outcome of my brother's life. It was so painful to be in that place again!

Well, the Lord knew exactly what I was thinking, and He decided that He would not allow me to sink into my despairing thoughts. As we were in the arcade playing, my daughter asked me to try a game. I did and immediately hit the jackpot and won 250 tickets! They were so excited because how often do you ever win enough tickets to actually get a decent prize in one of those places? So, we kept moving through the arcade, and they kept playing. When I found myself sinking again in my thoughts, my daughter said, "Try this one, mom!" I did, and immediately hit the jackpot again! The look in my girls' eyes was one of shock and pure excitement; it was contagious. They would try one, win a few tickets, and then ask me to play. Every time it was a jackpot! Before long they were asking me to try machine after machine. They were jumping up and down so excited! I was having so much fun with them that I was not able to sink into my thoughts anymore. It seemed like every time that I got close to doing it, we would hit another jackpot and win hundreds of tickets. They had a giant version of the claw game, a game using a mechanical claw to try to get a giant, stuffed animal. In the past, I had never had much luck in winning anything on those machines. They always seemed rigged to drop it, but my daughter insisted we try. To my surprise, we won a giant red dog! She was so happy, and, of course, it made me feel happy.

The friends we went with started to notice this strange stream of luck and followed us around for a bit; we looked at each other like somehow these machines were rigged. Out of tokens, we went to the counter with thousands of tickets (close to three thousand), and, for the first time ever in my arcade history, my kids were able to pick whatever toy they wanted.

Now, some people would say, "Big deal; you got lucky at an arcade.", but they don't know my Lord. You see, He knew what I had been through that year, He knew how hard it was for me to even enjoy being with my children because of the memories that flooded me while in that place. He made it to where every moment that my heart would start to sink I was immediately lifted up by the joy and the laughter in my kids. I couldn't despair in the midst of them jumping up and down squealing with excitement every time we hit a jackpot. For a few short hours, those games had been rigged because my God has a great sense of humor, and He knew exactly what I needed that day. He again reminded me that He sees me, knows me, and, yes, cares for me. The funny thing is my kids' memory of that day.

Another year later, we went there again. My kids' expectations of hitting the jackpot were so high! They were practically already picking out the toys they would get when they won thousands of tickets, so on the way there I had to talk to them and explain what had really happened that day. I told them how sad I had been about losing my brother (their uncle) that day and that God had encouraged me and blessed me with a fun day with them instead of letting me be sad. I also explained that it is not normal to hit the jackpot every time you play a game and that we shouldn't be disappointed when we don't. They both thought it was really great that God had done that for me that day when I was so sad, and they weren't disappointed later on when we won around 250 tickets like normal people, with no jackpots. However, now it is a very special memory that we share, the day God wouldn't let me be sad.

From 2013 to 2015, God did not take the darkness away. I was on a very painful journey of grief and loss. He didn't fix it all and stop the pain, but, instead, He used the pain to change me, to mold my character, to help me have compassion for others, and to be able to share my brother's story in juvenile hall to kids struggling with addictions. He faithfully and gently led me through that valley of the shadow of death without ever leaving my side for a moment. In my weakest moments, He revealed His strength because His power is truly made perfect in our weakness. Although the pain wasn't removed, His grace was sufficient to see me through to the end...and beyond.

Chapter 18
Pursuing Grace

"But now, O LORD, You are our Father;
we are the clay, and You are our potter;
we are all the work of Your hand."
Isaiah 64:8 (ESV)

September 2019, Grass Valley, California

HOW DID I GET HERE? I am a thirty-eight year-old Christian, wife, and a mother sitting here writing a book about my life. I never once thought I would live to see thirty, yet, here I am writing at nearly forty. I once thought there was no hope for my life, no future for me, that I would never be loved, never find happiness, never be married, and never have children. Yet, my life has become a series of the impossible becoming reality. So, why not write a book, too? After years of sharing what God has done in me and sharing my story in the local juvenile hall, people kept telling me, "You need to write a book!"

After praying and thinking about it for ten years, I finally decided to do it. It is no easy thing to share and expose your past. There are many things I would rather just stay in the past. Only this book isn't really just about my life; in fact, this story is not really about me, but it is about those moments that we all go through, those moments when we find ourselves in a place that we ask, "How did I get here?"

Sometimes our choices have brought us there; other times we had no choice, but we found ourselves in a place we cannot escape. I dare say, you know exactly what I am talking about; don't you? We all have been there. It is a course that seems to be pre-chosen for us, and we cannot explain how we got there. We only know that it is a pivotal moment in our lives, one that shakes us, changes us, and can even completely change our direction. Not every story is the same, yet we can all find ourselves in a place that seems to force us to rely on something other than ourselves, a place that is so full of desperation and so out of our control that we have no choice but to look up and cry out for help.

You see, our stories are all uniquely written, different from each other, yet, each life, each story, is a journey, and behind it all is the same Author. My story is actually about Him. I was the main player going my own way, thinking I was calling the shots and doing my own thing, yet all along He was behind the scenes directing the circumstances and using things to guide me to the path that led to Him. I can look back on so many moments that I should have died, the car that crashed a few feet from me, overdosing, being strangled until unconscious, and more, yet something protected me, something kept changing my direction even when I seemed so bent on self-destructing. Now, I know it was the Lord; it was always Him.

The Lord loved me so much that He never gave up on me even when I had given up on myself. He knew what it would take for me to finally admit that, if He was real, I needed Him. Because of how stubborn and prideful I was, not to mention angry, it took many years of breaking to get me there, yet He loved me enough to do it. I had to come to the end of every road. Each path was my attempt to run from Him, yet He loved me enough to let me do it so I would see it went nowhere. You see, His love is not the love of which we think. We think of a warm, fuzzy feeling we get when we love someone and want to give them everything good, but His is not like that. His love is unconditional, and it is not a mere feeling. His is an active and sacrificial love. His love cost Him everything, yet He was willing to give everything for us. There was no warm, fuzzy feeling in Him as He endured the cross of Calvary, yet He did it because He knew it was the payment we could never make for our sins. He knew we were His enemies and wanted nothing to do with Him, yet He still took our penalty, our shame, and our guilt upon Himself because He loved us. He loved me so much that He never allowed me to be truly happy in anything I did because He knew it was all empty, that it would never satisfy me, and that it was only temporary. Once I invited Him into my life, the missing piece was finally complete, the shame and guilt removed and the longing in my heart satisfied. Nothing can ever take that away. His love allowed me to suffer in my own ways because He knew that was what it would take to bring me to Him. I am so thankful for that kind of love, the kind that didn't give me what I wanted but what was the ultimate best for me.

When I was running from the pain, I was really running from His grace. His love and grace wanted to help me through the difficulties of life, but I saw them as control and ran from them. As a young girl, I started a cycle of running from the one thing that could have helped me through the pain, Him! Thankfully, His love and grace are faster than I ever could be and pursued me until I was caught, then carried me through the struggles and difficulties that still lay ahead of me in this life.

Today, I face new struggles, new challenges, and even some "How did I get here" moments, but I know He is with me and His grace is still sufficient to get me through them all until I make it home.

So what about your moments? Those moments in your story when you are wondering, "How did I get here?" Have you experienced a direction out of your control that seems to move and change the course of your life? Almost as though your story was already written and you are the main player going your own way, yet something is directing your path. Have you ever reached the point of looking up and saying, "God, if you are real, I need you."? Do you feel like you are carrying a burden that is too heavy to bear? Do you feel like you have been running, but you do not know what you're running from? Do you realize that He loves you just as much as He loves me? Do you realize that He will never allow you to be satisfied with the things that do not last so that you will hunger for the one thing that does, a relationship with Him? His love will pursue you; His grace is relentless. You can run from it like I did, or you can allow that love to catch you and transform you.

In Luke 15:11-32, Jesus shares the story of the prodigal son. He was a young man who left his home after asking for his inheritance, and he wasted it living for the things of this life. After much suffering, he returned to his home hoping to be made a servant because he didn't deserve to be called a son. Instead, His father was so happy that his son was alive and had returned that he showed him grace (undeserved blessing) and threw him a huge welcome home party.

I ran from the Lord for many years because life didn't go the way that I thought it should. I thought that if He were truly a God of love then my life wouldn't be so painful. Why was I poor? Why did my dad leave then die before I could meet him? Why would God allow my step dad to be so cruel? Why did I get raped? Why would no one really love me? I was angry and refused to believe in a God of love in a world that is so full of evil. I was angry at Him, so really I was running from God all along, which ultimately meant that I was running from His grace; I ran from the One thing that could've helped me, the One who actually loved me unconditionally, the One who was the answer for the questions I was searching. His love never ends; His love never fails. I know that now without a shadow of doubt.

Maybe you can relate with that; maybe your story has not gone the way that you thought it should. Maybe you are disappointed and hurt and have a hard time believing that God loves you. Really, for me, I was expecting heaven on earth. I wanted things good and perfect down here, and I blamed God when they did not go that way. Isn't it bizarre, myself and mankind chooses sin over God, yet we blame Him for the consequences of our sins—not very fair when you think about it.

Even so, none of that stops Him from pursuing us. He doesn't allow us to experience heaven now because He knows that this life is temporary and eternity comes next. He knows that if we leave this life without receiving His grace we will face judgment for the things we have done. (which is actually what is fair). Although He is a God of justice, He does not want justice for us. He knows we are guilty but instead wants to pardon us. He wants us to experience the real heaven, the place we all long for but do not know, a place free from the penalty of sin and death, a place where no one we love dies anymore, a place where no one is sick, nor suffers—a real life, eternal life. He also knows that the decision to receive His forgiveness and grace must be made in our lifetime. No wonder He pursues us! No wonder He doesn't allow us to be too comfortable here! No wonder He allows us to experience the things this world has to offer so we see they are empty things, void of meaning and unsatisfying. He allows us to pursue things this world says are valuable so in the end we see they are not. He wants us to hunger and thirst for the things that do satisfy us so we will pursue it the way He has pursued us all along.

In my story, I now know that all that pain, all that heartache that I experienced before I gave my life to Christ were all tools He was using to bring me to the end of myself, so He could begin to write a new story in me. He took a beaten up, broken, and abused drug addict and made me new. He cleansed me, healed me, and started a whole new story in me—one of love and value, fruitful and cherished by the Creator. There is still heartache, struggle, and pain in that new story, but the difference is amazing. When life gets hard, I get to see my God move on my behalf. When challenges are great and too big for me, I get to see how trustworthy the Lord really is and that He never fails. When heartbreak takes over, I get to experience the God of all comfort like I had never known before. Now the difficulties do not make me angry; instead, I know they are God's opportunities to reveal Himself to me in new ways, more secrets we get to share together, His chance to mold me and shape my character, His tool to make me a more loving and compassionate person because other people are suffering everyday.

A year after my brother's death, I wrote this in my journal:

"Life is full of curveballs. There are highs and lows, and the path is littered with disappointments. The challenges and obstacles can come so frequently that sometimes there seems to be no end. So, what do you do? You cannot give up; you certainly don't want to go backwards after working so hard to get here. Do you stop moving forward? Stand still? You could try, but life would keep coming at you, pushing you backwards. No, there is only one way; you push forward, leaving the disappointments wherever they lay, moving on, and relying on the Lord to guide each step and to light the path in front of your feet. Trusting that He knows what awaits you in the dark and will give you what you need once you are there and not a moment before. Resting in the fact that one day the race will be over and then you will stop running. Until then, push, climb, fight, do whatever you must just keep moving forward. When it is all over, you will see that the path littered with disappointments, if surrendered to Christ will become His fruitful orchard. A path so beautiful and sweet, covered with an abundant harvest that fed every soul that crossed its path. All that we faced, all we let go of was not just for us. No trial was wasted, no obstacle accidental, all a part of His marvelous plan for His beloved...you."

I hope and pray that after reading this story, my story about His story, that you realize how important your story really is. I hope that you know and understand that your loving Creator knows you, understands you, and pursues you with His love and grace whether you realize it yet or not. He knows that your eternity is at stake, and He won't stop drawing you and trying to get your attention. He will never allow things to be perfect here because this is not our permanent home; we are just passing through this life. He knows what you have suffered and doesn't want you to have to suffer beyond this life, He will use all you have endured for good, and bring you to Him. He knows that without Him you are incomplete; He made you that way so you would seek Him. I also hope that as you have found yourself reading this book that you have asked yourself the question, "How did I get here?" Maybe now, you will know the Answer.

So, what now?

If you have never accepted Jesus Christ as your Lord and Savior and have never received His free gift of salvation, but you want to, please let me share with you how.

I am sure by now you realize that you are not perfect, that, in fact, you are a sinner. Truth is, you were born that way; we are all born sinners. *(Psalm 51:5 "Behold, I was brought forth in iniquity,and in sin did my mother conceive me." ESV)* That is not your fault. By one man, Adam, the first created man in the Garden of Eden, sin came into the world. *(Romans 5:12 "Therefore, just as sin came into the world through one man, and death through sin, and so death spread to all men because all sinned."ESV)*

However, later you showed that you were, in fact, a sinner by the choices you made; that makes you guilty, your own choices. *(Romans 3:23 "for all have sinned and fall short of the glory of God." ESV)*

We have all broken God's moral laws (Ten Commandments), even if you have never heard them. Scripture says they are written on our hearts *(Romans 2:15 "They show that the work of the law is written on their hearts, while their conscience also bears witness, and their conflicting thoughts accuse or even excuse them." ESV)*; that is how we know when we have done something wrong without someone even telling us.

So, that puts all mankind in a bad spot...guilty! Breakers of God's moral law! As lawbreakers, the Bible teaches that our sin makes us enemies of God *(Romans 5:10a "For if while we were enemies we were reconciled to God by the death of his Son." ESV)* and that the wages of sin is death *(Romans 6:23a "For the wages of sin is death." ESV)* That is the bad news.

The good news is that Jesus paid the debt for your sin, the cost of our guilt. *(Romans 6:23 "For the wages of sin is death, but the free gift of God is eternal life in Christ Jesus our Lord." ESV)* God made provision–just like sin entered into the world by one man (Adam), by one man, Jesus Christ, the penalty (or payment/wages) of sin – death –is paid for *(Romans 5:17 "For if, because of one man's trespass, death reigned through that one man, much more will those who receive the abundance of grace and the free gift of righteousness reign in life through the one man Jesus Christ." ESV)*

His gift was to pay the debt we earned. He paid it in full by giving His life. He was the perfect sacrifice for sin because He never sinned! *(John 1:29 "Behold, the Lamb of God, who takes away the sin of the world!", 2 Corinthians 5:21 "For our sake he made him to be sin who knew no sin, so that in him we might become the righteousness of God." ESV)* His gift of eternal life is a free gift to mankind. You do not earn it; you cannot buy it; you cannot do enough good deeds to obtain it;it is a gift to receive or decline. That is up to you. His gift will only benefit you if you apply it to your account by receiving it.

According to the Bible, this is what you need to do if you want His payment (His gift of salvation) to cancel the debt you owe:

- Pray; talk to Him

- Acknowledge that you are a sinner, that you need His mercy.

- Ask Him to forgive your sins...all of them!

- Tell Him that you believe Jesus is God and that He died in your place.

- Tell Him that you want Him to be the Lord of your life and you want to live for Him.

- Ask Him to fill you with His Spirit and give you the strength to live for Him.

- Then, thank Him for His free gift of eternal life!!! (*Romans 10:9-10 "because, if you <u>confess</u> with your mouth that Jesus is Lord and <u>believe</u> in your heart that God raised him from the dead, <u>you will be saved.</u> For with the heart one believes and is justified, and with the mouth one confesses and is saved." ESV*)

Or you can say a simple prayer like this one:
Lord, I admit I am a sinner. I need and want Your forgiveness. I accept Your death as the penalty for my sin, and recognize that Your mercy and grace is a gift You offer to me because of Your great love, not based on anything I have done. Cleanse me and make me Your child.

Sounds simple? It is! It has to be. If it were complicated, we would mess it up.

Once you've received God's free gift of eternal life and payment for your debt (sins) has been applied to your account, it belongs to you. No one can take it from you, and no one can take you from the almighty hands of God! That is why it is called eternal life. (*John 3:16 "For God so loved the world, that he gave his only Son, that whoever believes in him should not perish but have eternal life.",*

John 10:28-29 "I give them eternal life, and they will never perish, and no one will snatch them out of my hand. My Father, who has given them to me, is greater than all, and no one is able to snatch them out of the Father's hand." ESV)

Jesus is a perfect gentleman, and He will never force anyone to take His offer. He only offers it freely to the "...*whoever believes in Him [so that they] should not perish but have eternal life*" (*John 3:16*)

Once you have received that free gift, your debt has been paid in full. You now have peace with God. (*Romans 5:1 "Therefore, since we have been justified by faith, we have peace with God through our Lord Jesus Christ." ESV*) Meaning, if you died today, you could stand before a holy and just God...forgiven and cleared of all charges! Even though you were declared guilty previously.

It doesn't end there though. You see, God not only wants to give you mercy (not giving you what you deserve), but He also wants to extend you grace (undeserved blessing; giving us what we don't deserve).

By accepting His free gift, you become a child of God. *(John 1:12 "But to all who did receive him, who believed in his name, he gave the right to become children of God" ESV)* You have been adopted into His family *(Romans 8:14 "For all who are led by the Spirit of God are sons of God." ESV)*

Some would say, "Great! My sin is paid for; I can live any way I want, including going back to my sin!" However, that is not His will for you. Would a slave go back to slavery after being set free? No! Neither should you...a child of God! *(Galatians 4:7 So you are no longer a slave, but a son, and if a son, then an heir through God. ESV)* Sadly, like my brother Matt we are capable of choosing slavery over freedom even after receiving salvation. The choice of who we will serve is still ours to make everyday and the consequences come with it. Jesus wants you free, Satan wants you in bondage to sin.

You see, sin made us slaves; Jesus set us free. *(John 8:34 "Jesus answered them, "Truly, truly, I say to you, everyone who practices sin is a slave to sin. 36 So if the Son sets you free, you will be free indeed." ESV)*

You are now free to live for Him and experience a personal relationship with the true and living God, something you couldn't do before because of the sin that had separated you from Him. *(Isaiah 59:2 "But your iniquities have separated you from your God; And your sins have hidden His face from you, So that He will not hear." ESV)*

As His child, you are now free to say no to sin (something you couldn't do before), free to allow Him to use you in your life to do good *(Ephesians 2:10 "For we are his workmanship, created in Christ Jesus for good works, which God prepared beforehand, that we should walk in them." ESV)*, free to be a light bearer by helping others find their way out of the dark. *(Matthew 5:14-16 "You are the light of the world. A city set on a hill cannot be hidden. Nor do people light a lamp and put it under a basket, but on a stand, and it gives light to all in the house. In the same way, let your light shine before others, so that they may see your good works and give glory to your Father who is in heaven." ESV)*

Please!

Find a Bible believing church and get plugged into the family of Christ right away! *(Hebrews 10:25 "not neglecting to meet together, as is the habit of some, but encouraging one another, and all the more as you see the Day drawing near." ESV)*

Get a Bible, and allow God to speak to you through His living word...it will be food for your soul. Eat it often! *(Hebrews 4:12 "For the word of God is living and active, sharper than any two-edged sword, piercing to the division of soul and of spirit, of joints and of marrow, and discerning the thoughts and intentions of the heart." ESV)*

Speak to Him everyday, acknowledging His presence in your life; thanking Him for His gift of salvation, His protection, and His provisions; and talking to Him (maybe, even asking for help), thus maintaining a relationship, because you now have access to the creator of the Universe! Use it! *(Hebrews 4:16 "Let us then with confidence draw near to the throne of grace, that we may receive mercy and find grace to help in time of need." ESV)*

Know this, your life will never be the same, you are now in the hands of the Potter *(Isaiah 64:8 "But now, O LORD, you are our Father; we are the clay, and you are our potter; we are all the work of your hand." ESV)*; He will mold you into something beautiful, something useful and valuable and He will never let you go. You are His, He will take care of you as He sees best.

Although the road ahead can be difficult (Earth is not Heaven!), He does promise this: *Romans 8:28 And we know that for those who love God all things work together for good, for those who are called according to his purpose. (ESV)*

If you truly meant from your heart what you said in prayer above, you are now "called according to His purposes!" That means that no matter what difficulty you face, God PROMISES He will use it for good in your story, in your life. I can bear witness to that, and to the fact that He NEVER breaks His promises!

Until we meet at "home", dear friend, God bless you! Please, shine brightly so others can see the way out of the darkness...always remember that others need to be set free, too, so never keep the gift all to yourself. If this book has encouraged you in any way, please give it to someone who needs to hear that there is hope in this crazy world and they are not alone. Let's share the hope of Christ with whoever we can, while we still can.

Your Sister IN Christ,
Joy Sidebottom

9 7 9 8 2 2 3 3 4 8 5 6 6